The Frantic Assembly

Book of Devising Theatre

SCOTT GRAHAM AND STEVEN HOGGETT

Routledge
Taylor & Francis Group

LONDON AND NEW YORK

First published 2009 by Routledge
2 Park Square, Milton Park, Abingdon, Oxon OX14 4RN

Simultaneously published in the USA and Canada
by Routledge
270 Madison Avenue, New York, NY 10016

Reprinted 2009, 2010

Routledge is an imprint of the Taylor & Francis Group, an informa business

© 2009 Scott Graham and Steven Hoggett

All photographs © Scott Graham, unless otherwise credited

Typeset in Univers by
Keystroke, 28 High Street, Tettenhall, Wolverhampton

Printed and bound in Great Britain by
CPI Antony Rowe, Chippenham, Wiltshire

British Library Cataloguing in Publication Data
A catalogue record for this book is available from the British Library

Library of Congress Cataloging in Publication Data
Graham, Scott, 1971-
    The Frantic Assembly : book of devising theatre / Scott Graham and
    Steven Hoggett.
        p. cm.
    Includes bibliographical references.
    1. Frantic Assembly (Group) 2. Experimental theater—Great Britain.
    3. Theatrical companies—Great Britain. 4. Improvisation (Acting)
    5. Movement (Acting) I. Hoggett, Steven, 1971– II. Title.
    III. Title: Frantic Assembly book of devising theatre.
    PN2595.13E97G73 2009
    792.0941—dc22   2008043559

ISBN13: 978–0–415–46536–6 (hbk)
ISBN13: 978–0–415–46760–5 (pbk)

ISBN10: 0–415–46536–2 (hbk)
ISBN10: 0–415–46760–8 (pbk)

The Frantic Assembly

Book of Devising Theatre

Acclaimed by audiences and critics for their highly innovative and adventurous theatre, Frantic Assembly have created playful, intelligent and dynamic productions for over 14 years. *The Frantic Assembly Book of Devising Theatre* is written by artistic directors Scott Graham and Steven Hoggett. It is the first book to reflect on the history and practice of this remarkable company, and includes:

- practical exercises
- essays on devising, writing and choreography
- suggestions for scene development
- an anthology of Frantic Assembly productions
- an eight-page colour section, and illustrations throughout.

This intimate and personal account offers an accessible, educational and indispensable introduction to the evolution and success of Frantic Assembly. It is also accompanied by a companion website featuring clips of rehearsals and performances.

Scott Graham and Steven Hoggett are the artistic directors and co-founders of Frantic Assembly.

This book is dedicated to the following:

Liz Heywood for seeing something at the very start – thank you
Sally Harris for *teaching us everything you knew!*
Sian, Marcia and Carys Graham

Contents

CONTENTS

Acknowledgements

In our experience, Frantic Assembly has been exactly that – a frantic blast through some astounding experiences surrounded by an assembly of wonderful people.

Notable frantic companions are Lisa Maguire, Laura Sutton, Tom Morris, Ben and Claire Chamberlain, Vicky Featherstone, John Tiffany, Georgina Lamb, Natasha Chivers, Liam Steel, Simon Mellor, Dan O'Neill, Simon Stokes, David Sibley, Spencer Hazel, Korina Biggs, Cait Davis, and our families.

We were only ever as fine as our product and to this end we have been blessed with the cast and creative teams behind the Frantic productions – a fearless and inspiring group of artists who represent the very best in creative generosity and spirit.

Special mention to Vicki Middleton (née Coles), the vital element in our unholy trinity. The three of us formed the company and stumbled through the first ten years before she was whisked off to Australia with a promise of sunshine, surf and snags on the barbie.

All of the above allowed and encouraged us to be what we are and for that we truly love and thank you.

And thanks to Talia Rodgers . . . for the suggestion, the encouragement, and the patience.

An introduction

A very brief history of Frantic Assembly

This book is not about the history of our company, but a little background information might explain a lot about our company ethos. The nature of how we came to be has been a massive influence on our drive to make our work accessible. It has informed all our efforts in education and training.

As English Literature students at Swansea University we met as an unused understudy and a bored stage manager on a student drama society production of *Educating Rita*. Swansea University does not have a drama department but it does have a fantastic theatre that hosts the drama society three or four times a year presenting the usual talcum powder headed Chekhov and vanity projects. That is what we thought theatre was.

As students we respectively took part in and watched a student production directed by Volcano Theatre Company (*Savages* by Christopher Hampton). This was the life-changing moment. We did not know that theatre could be like this. We had experienced this production from both sides of the fourth wall and it had blown our preconceptions apart. It was also clear that this was what we both wanted to do with our lives.

Volcano were a massive inspiration to us. They were alternative and sexy, intelligent and fierce. They were the perfect role models for us, being Politics and Psychology graduates from Swansea who had been inspired by another director to set their company up and create their own work. They recognised the inspiration and expertise they could give us and actively encouraged, advised and nurtured us during the early days. This is why our education and training programmes are so important to us.

With Volcano's encouragement we presented *Savages* at the Edinburgh Fringe Festival. For 'we' you should read 'Swansea University Drama Society'. Before signing up for the festival we were to be found huddled around a thesaurus trying to agree on a company name. For some reason we felt that Swansea University Drama Society was not going to bring the punters in. We all agreed on Chaos then found out there was a Kaos Theatre Company. Then someone proposed Frantic and Frantic it was.

The next year we directed *As Is* by William M. Hoffman and took it to Edinburgh, again as Frantic Theatre Company. We managed to sell out both runs and garner good national reviews. It was felt that if we could fool the public so far, maybe we should give it a go full time. That is when Vicki Middleton (née Coles), Scott Graham and Steven Hoggett decided to hatch a plan and turn a hobby into a career.

We got other (proper) jobs for the year while we waited for each other to finish our studies before returning to Swansea to start the company officially. The reason for starting out in Swansea had everything to do with Volcano, the goodwill and encouragement of those at the Taliesin Arts Centre, the lower cost of living, and the prospect of immediately being a small fish in a small pond. We felt that in being anywhere else, even Cardiff, we would get swamped in the clamour for new companies to get noticed.

We formed the company proper under the name Frantic Theatre Company Limited in 1994 on a government scheme called Enterprise Allowance. In real terms this meant being unemployed for at least 6 weeks and taking a £10 pay cut from your Jobseeker's Allowance and attending seminars and meetings on finance and business. Being on the scheme meant that we did not have to sign on at the job centre for the year as we built the business up. Enterprise Allowance contributed £30 a week to each of our wages and the company added another £10.

We had decided that our approach to building the company would be all or nothing. We would not get part-time jobs so that we could concentrate fully on Frantic. This mostly meant tapping out letters to venue programmers on an old typewriter, stuffing envelopes and waiting for the phone to ring.

Our first tour saw us take a radical reworking of *Look Back in Anger* to mystified audiences in arts centres throughout Wales and a few dates in England. With each production came an intense learning curve gained from working with a talented freelance choreographer. Their input was our training. We had little more to offer than boundless energy and enthusiasm (which of course should never be underestimated). We were also brave and driven in our desire to both try new things and make an impact on the theatrical world. *Look Back in Anger* was our way in.

The book

Is it possible to work within a specific field for over 14 years and still feel like there is so much left to discover, that the tag of 'expert' is still something on the far horizon? We would be the first to answer with a resounding 'yes'. Talking with Rufus Norris during the making of *Market Boy* at the National Theatre in spring 2006 we all confessed to traces of anxiety regarding our title as directors. Despite it being what we wrote down on official forms such as visa applications and dentists' registration forms, we realised that the time when we least felt like directors in any given year would be the time actually spent in the rehearsal room. Short on long spells in therapy, we still haven't managed to solve this issue. At the time of writing, Rufus has shown no signs of recovery either.

There is a definite 'Next!' mentality to the way in which Frantic Assembly operates, a desire to keep pushing forwards. As two people with famously short attention spans, this may be one of the reasons we are still doing what we do in the way that we do it. That we have created 16 full-scale productions in these 14 years is testament to this mentality and practice. This does not mean, however, that our approach and thinking is in a state of constant change and flux.

Writing this book has been a fascinating exercise for us. For the most part, we have always maintained that we define ourselves best by stating what we are not. This book has forced us to assume the opposite and lay it down in a way that makes sense. The result is a truly empirical account of what it is to create devised theatre in Britain today. The contents are formed by those practices that, for us, have been some kind of constant or consistency over the years – practice that still holds true in identifying what it is that makes Frantic theatre Frantic. For this very reason, there are many episodes, events and discoveries that you will not find in this book. Experiments with dried flowers and petroleum in a flammable dressing room and the resultant effect. Sets that, mid-performance, collapse and land on the feet of the performers. All are episodes best left to the ages and in no way can be called upon to represent good practice. That there are enough instances like this to fill another book should in no way deter the reader from following the thinking and ideas contained here. On the contrary, we would like to think that our careers being littered with an expansive array of mistakes makes us informed and trustworthy in describing the trials and tribulations of modern theatre making. It is unlikely that anyone else can, with authority, advise what to do when you mistakenly pull down your pants in front of a sell-out home crowd during a premiere. But like we say, that's another book altogether.

What you will find here is a determined effort to demystify the devising process. To this end, the book falls into two parts. The first is a selection of scenes that cover the creative output of the company from early shows such as *Klub* through to *Stockholm*. Each of these scenes is taken and examined in terms of the initial idea followed by the methods used in transferring that idea from a scrap of conversation or grotty notebook into the production and onto the stage. We then look at possible ways in which this existing scene might be developed or how the creative process could be harnessed to create something different. The second part expresses our belief that the reader should not think about the ideas here being an end point. When running workshops, we are always at pains to point out to participants that the most important part to take away from the workshop is not the creative end point we might have reached but the means by which we got there. It is the understanding of the process that is valuable. We are certainly not unique in being a company who continues to work on the production throughout its tour. The development of ideas is essential once the production begins to seek validity in front of an audience.

Part One also includes a number of essays that cover some of the elements and ideas central to the Frantic method of thinking about and creating theatre (see Chapter 1). As well as revealing the places where we find ideas and inspiration, it is hoped that this chapter might encourage the practitioner to reconsider their own inspirational locations and, in doing so, free up the frequently self-imposed restrictions on where to be looking for creative motivation. Part One also covers specifics of our practice such as why we used our own names on stage for so long and why the pre-show state is so important to us.

Part Two is a comprehensive guide through the creation of physical theatre, starting with warm-up advice and games through to advanced choreographic exercises before looking at specific uses of music and text in our theatre practice. Each exercise has been tried and tested by the company over a number of years working with a wide variety of practitioners ranging in age and ability.

We hope that the reader of this book will find enough points of interest to instigate their own search for good practice. In our own experience, it has been important to establish both starting points and departure points for ourselves. This book should work in the same way – a healthy balance of agreeable and disagreeable pointers, thoughts, exercises and suggestions. It is an attempt to provoke the reader into looking for new means of creating theatre performance. Our own non-theatre background meant that we had no choice but to forge our own understanding of how to create work. This in itself might have been a blessing as we have never felt beholden to any particular school of thought or theatrical tradition. A rigid sense of what theatre should be will always be the enemy of devised theatre. The 'what might be' is essential.

An introduction will usually go to great lengths to define the terms central to the book. Sorry, but we are not really interested in this. Having spent years wrestling with the term 'physical theatre', we finally gave ourselves licence to leave that job to academics and commentators and people much better placed to offer definitions and devote our time to getting on with the job of making theatre. It might be argued that all theatre is physical and that all theatre is, to some extent, devised. That argument is not one we care about enough to dedicate space to here. It is a waste of precious time. Let's just get on with it! We encourage practitioners to get into the rehearsal room, make the work and let the audience be the ones to speculate on what it is they just experienced.

OK, OK, we will talk about physical theatre. Later. Let's talk about devising first.

What devising means to us

We have produced 16 full-scale productions in 14 years. Add to this the dozen or so short performance pieces developed with students over the years as residencies and the artistic output of the company is, if nothing else, constant. In an age where some artists and companies seek to refine and develop work over a number of years, we have always been of the mind that an essential form of development is the next production. We really do not know what we have learnt from the last production until we are under the pressure of making a new production.

It is possible to imagine that devising implies that we have gone into a room with nothing and tried to make a start from scratch. This is not the case. It may take years for an idea to get into the rehearsal room and before it does it has been batted back and forth between the directors, reshaped and presented to producers and other collaborators. It has been presented to a writer too, who may be engaged to create a full draft for the first day of rehearsal. That script becomes the launch pad and inspiration for most of the devising process.

As we develop our rehearsal processes we have been taking advantage of the generous opportunities to try out ideas through the help of institutions such as the National Theatre Studio or BAC. This is much more like the precon-ception of devising but it is without the reductive pressure of existing within a dwindling rehearsal time. It is focused and disciplined but it is definitely the time to be playing with 'what if?' This research and development can be physically led, or it could be about developing story and text. We might explore character work either textually or physically, but all work will be within a clearly defined subject. We would have talked about our aims and created techniques to explore them, partly wanting to be proved successful and partly wanting to be surprised by the outcome.

The point here is that we have refined and adapted this approach to making theatre over the years. We initially create the kernel of the idea and test this to see if it is interesting enough to us and if 'it has got legs' – whether it will stand up to scrutiny and be interesting to anyone else. This 'testing' is pretty much talking about the idea, letting it sit for a while and then returning to it with a wiser head to see if it still excites us.

We then take it into development with as many of our collaborators as possible on board. Here we flesh it out and hopefully come out with a much bigger idea that would then go into the rehearsal stage where a full script would be presented. Despite all this, it is important to state that we are no heroes of process. There are those artists who will argue that the value of process is as important, if not more so than, the value of result. This line of thinking seems to forget that the main point of creativity in theatre is about the end point, the public event. At this moment of presentation what is crucial is the result. True, a secondary response from an audience might be along the lines of 'how did they end up making this thing?' and one would hope that such questioning would be the result of an audience marvelling at the wonder in front of them. It is only right to admit that the same question is often the first in our minds when viewing some of the theatrical horrors we have had the misfortune to witness over the years. Ultimately, we firmly support the audience member's right to pay for product over process. Any other set-up needs to involve a very generous refund policy.

Devising is not to the exclusion of working with a writer. And that writer has to be allowed the freedom to develop a text and not just be expected to be inspired by what is created in the rehearsal room. In eschewing the practice of plucking an existing script off the shelf, a creative team sometimes needs to be reminded that this is an act of creative freedom. On dark days this can seem like anything but. At such times it is important to remember that the rehearsal process is a totally non-linear event. Half of your ideas will not have come to fruition halfway through the rehearsals and it is unlikely that in the third week of a four-week rehearsal schedule you will be sat on 75 percent of the finished product. Most rehearsals are a haphazard cumulative event where clarity and creativity collectively form half the requisite qualities. The other half requires you to hold your nerve. At various times throughout our career we have been great at this. At other times, the lack has caused us great anguish and severe doubt. The ability to hold one's nerve is affected not only by the state of affairs within the room, but also personal lives, the prevailing cultural climate at the time, the well-being of the producing company, the tenacity and interrelationships within the creative team. But there is nothing more satisfying than emerging from the very frontier of chaos and returning with something beyond the artistic expectations of the rehearsal process.

All of our devising is broken down into tasks. These remain bite sized and self-contained. They never set out to encapsulate the whole production idea or solve the entire demands of the text. They are always as simple as we can make them as they are merely building blocks, created to support more blocks. A task might be as simple as asking one performer to hide 15 Post-it notes around a kitchen and then setting the other performer the task of finding them while the rest of the company watch the latter's response. This exercise, used as part of rehearsals for *Stockholm*, was to have a profound effect on our understanding of the history between two incredibly complex characters. By setting tasks you allow your performers to offer much creative input into the devising of choreography without burdening them with the responsibility of creating the whole show. Such burdening may not bring out the best in your performer. The shaping of theatre and choreography requires an outside eye and it is this objective influence that can liberate the performer to be brave, take risks and try things new. We, as the directors/choreographers, are liberated too as the performer is now providing a palette so much larger and richer than our own imaginations could provide. We feel this relationship and process sets both performers and directors free to use their full imaginations as well as working with ideas we would never have thought about.

We are firm believers that limitations create freedoms and breed creativity. We are certainly not for the suffering of the artist. Asking performers to improvise in a void can be really counterproductive. It is the pain of personal experience that has shaped this approach as well as the influence and approaches of the very talented choreographers we have worked with. They recognised the need to simplify things for us, to see what we could do and then use this. We responded to their use of rules and parameters and have taken this process on as our own. This is probably why we never teach choreography from the front of the room. In rehearsals we never teach 'steps'. The moves come from what the performers find they are capable of through the specific tasks set. We believe this is the most productive, honest and accessible method for us.

Despite never going into a rehearsal room without some form of solid intention, a significant part of devising is to not know. We do not walk into rehearsals on day one clutching a big black notebook full of all the answers. At best, that notebook will contain some images, possibly a list of song titles, sketchy descriptions of images without a linking factor between them, possibly a few quotes and lots and lots of clean white space. Another vital component is to agree to trust one another. Surprisingly, this is not always a condition that automatically gets easier the longer you work with another creative. Nor is it impossible to create this state among a group of total creative strangers. It will, of course, depend on the attitudes and abilities of the individuals involved and for this reason it is essential to work with a gut instinct when putting together a devising team. Nothing else is of any value in making this kind of decision.

Our favourite devising processes are the ones where the lines of creativity start to blur. A successful production for us will be one where it is hard to distinguish which came first between, say, words and movement or movement and music. This is achieved in a rehearsal room where the creative team act as one unit, sitting in front of the same scene or image or moment and all feeding into the process not just as, say, lighting designer but as a potential audience member and a Frantic theatre maker.

During a development period for *Stockholm*, we invited Martin Holbraad, an anthropologist at University College London, to spend the week in the room with us. To begin with there was no agenda as there was no notion as to what might be of interest for anthropological study. As a company, we were simply inquisitive as to how our creative process was seen to operate from the outside and how we might look to adapt or improve it. One interesting observation Martin made was our constant use of anecdotes and break-outs into story-telling. It was noted that these alternative templates were all about creating an environment of anti-pretentiousness. Following this observation through in a conversation, we talked about how it feels counterproductive for us to allow the individual to go solo within the rehearsal room for too long. A certain strain of individualism seemed to have no place within the Frantic rehearsal room. The practice of sharing was critical to the working dynamic. This led Martin to conclude that 'membership of the group [was] openness'. In considering what are the ideal conditions for devising theatre, this sentiment is one that we believe sits at the very heart of our understanding and practice of devising theatre.

Anthology of work

Throughout this book we may refer to productions, scenes and practitioners, particularly in Chapter 2, 'Scenes and their creation'. It only seems fair to introduce you to the work at this stage. What follows is an anthology of the full-scale productions, a few words about them and a list of some of the people involved in their creation. They are set out in chronological order. Hopefully this will make things clearer as you progress through this book. Feel free to dip in and out. (Cast names are those of original performers. Names that appear in brackets replaced the original performers for part of the tour.)

Scott Graham and Steven Hoggett © David Sibley

Look Back in Anger   1994

Adapted by Spencer Hazel
Directed by Juan M. Carroscoso
Designed by Steven Hoggett
Lighting design by Spencer Hazel

Cast: Korina Biggs, Claire Evetts (Emily Jenkins, Alison Forth), Scott Graham, Steven Hoggett (Spencer Hazel)

Putting the fire back into the angry young man, this was a highly stylised inter-pretation. This was stripped down to the principal characters and presented the flat they shared as an emotional bear pit, a cruel arena of both overt and passive aggression.

UK tour, Edinburgh Fringe Festival

Klub 1995

Devised
Text by Spencer Hazel
Choreography by Stephen Kirkham
Lighting design by Spencer Hazel

Cast: Korina Biggs, Lucy McClellan (Cait Davis), Scott Graham, Spencer Hazel, Steven Hoggett (Roy Fears), Karina Sarmiento (Georgina Lamb)

Klub was a highly physical delve into club culture at a time when it was being squeezed from all sides, from the drug-related death of Leah Betts to the commercialisation of the clubbing experience. Six loosely linked characters embark on a good night out at all costs, each betraying their needs from the clubbing sensation as well as their desires for more than this.

Two UK tours, Ecuador, Egypt, Edinburgh Fringe Festival

Flesh 1996

Devised
Text by Spencer Hazel
Choreography by Christine Devaney
Designed by the company
Lighting design by Spencer Hazel

Cast: Korina Biggs, Cait Davis, Scott Graham, Steven Hoggett

Covering all aspects of selling your body for profit, *Flesh* touched on the nature of performance, prostitution and our obsession with mortality.

Two UK tours, Germany, Italy, Hungary, Spain,
two Netherlands tours, Edinburgh Fringe Festival

Devised and written by the company
Choreography by Steve Kirkham
Lighting design by Scott Graham

Cast: Korina Biggs, Cait Davis, Scott Graham, Steven Hoggett, Georgina Lamb

A photograph is taken in a house party on New Year's Eve 1999. It is a time for thought. Am I where I thought I would be now? And what about the future? *Zero* tackled and predicted pre-millennium tension.

> *Premiered at the 1998 Edinburgh Festival and toured the UK, Holland, Switzerland, Austria, Singapore and Hungary*

Klub, Flesh *and* Zero *were sometimes referred to as the Generation Trilogy which was performed in its entirety in Manchester, London and Exeter in spring 1998.*

Written by Michael Wynne
Choreography by T. C. Howard
Designed by Scott Graham and Steven Hoggett
Lighting design by Natasha Chivers

Cast: Cait Davis, Scott Graham (Craig Cremin), Steven Hoggett, Anstey Thomas

An argument grows from an honest word among friends. And it grows quickly. *Sell Out* starts with a whisper, snowballing to an irresistible force spiralling out of control.

> *A UK tour culminated in a West End run at the New Ambassadors Theatre.* Sell Out *won the Time Out Live Theatre Best Off West End Award. Toured Finland, France, Zimbabwe, Lebanon, Syria and Ireland*

Original production comissioned by the Gantry, Southampton Arts
   Centre and produced in association with Lyric Hammersmith
Written by Chris O'Connell
Directed and choreographed by Liam Steel
Designed by Liam Steel
Lighting design by Natasha Chivers

Cast: Scott Graham (Eddie Kay), Steven Hoggett, Simon Rees (Joseph
Traynor), Karl Sullivan (Liam Steel)

Set after the funeral of a mutual friend, what starts as small talk and banter
becomes a sadistic hunt for weakness, as four friends push each other until
something snaps.

Toured the UK, London, Columbia,
Italy, Ireland and Taiwan

Written by Nicola McCartney
Directed by Scott Graham and Steven Hoggett
Choreography by T. C. Howard
Designed by Scott Graham and Steven Hoggett
Lighting design by Jonathan Clark

Cast: Lydia Baksh, Sarah Beard, Georgina Lamb, Marcia Pook (Susannah
Cave)

Hard, dark, fast and frightening, *Underworld* was a ghost story for the twenty-
first century with a mix of touching realism and bruising physicality. It was also
the first Frantic show where the Artistic Directors of the company did not also
perform.

Toured the UK, London and Slovakia

Paines Plough and Frantic Assembly with Contact, Manchester
Written by Abi Morgan
Directed by Vicky Featherstone with Scott Graham and Steven Hoggett
Designed by Julian Crouch
Lighting design by Natasha Chivers
Music by Nick Powell

Cast: Scott Graham (Burn Gorman), Steven Hoggett, Jasmine Hyde (Leslie Hart, Sarah Beard, Eileen Walsh)

An impossible love story is given a second chance and three scorched characters learn that lightning does strike twice.

Winner of Best Fringe Production, Manchester Evening News Awards and Best Theatre Show, City Life Magazine. Toured UK, Edinburgh Festival, London, Bulgaria, Lithuania, Slovenia, Macedonia, Finland and Italy

Co-production with Drum Theatre Plymouth
Written and directed by Scott Graham, Steven Hoggett and Liam Steel
Choreographed by Liam Steel with Scott Graham and Steven Hoggett
Designed by Dick Bird
Lighting design by Colin Grenfell
Music by Nathaniel Reid

Cast: Scott Graham, Steven Hoggett and Liam Steel

Two brothers and a friend find themselves in a waiting room in Heaven after a drunken New Year's Eve quest for love along a rugged coastal path. But things are not that simple. It seems the room is trying to tell them that one of them should not be there.

UK tour and Off Broadway New York

Co-production with Drum Theatre Plymouth and Lyric Hammersmith
Written by Isobel Wright
Directed by Scott Graham and Steven Hoggett
Choreographed by Dan O'Neill with Scott Graham and Steven Hoggett
Design by Dick Bird
Lighting design by Natasha Chivers
Music by lamb
Musical direction by Nicholas Skilbeck

Cast: Kate Alderton, Sarah Beard, Richard Dempsey, Sharon Duncan-Brewster, Ben Joiner, Georgina Lamb, Richard Mylan

Inspired by the music video, especially a Michel Gondry video for Massive Attack, *Peepshow* showed the lives of people living in a block of flats and how those lives interconnect.

UK tour

A Frantic Assembly and Drum Theatre, Plymouth production supported
   by Lakeside Arts Centre
Written by Brendan Cowell
Directed and choreographed by Scott Graham and Steven Hoggett
Design by Dick Bird
Lighting design by Guisseppe di Lorio
Music by Deadly Avenger

Cast: Sam Crane, Helen Heaslip, Sue Kyd, David Sibley, Karl Sullivan

Mum and Dad are about to arrive and Madeleine and Spin are not so elegantly wasted. But that does not matter as Madeleine is going to give her father some home truths. What she does not know is that he also has something to say that is really going to rock her world.

UK Tour

A Frantic Assembly, Paines Plough and Graeae production
Written by Glyn Cannon
Directed by Vicky Featherstone, Scott Graham, Steven Hoggett and
    Jenny Sealey
Design by Julian Crouch
Lighting design by Natasha Chivers
Music by Nick Powell

Cast: Mat Fraser, Scott Graham, Steven Hoggett, Karina Jones, Jo
McInnes, David Sands

Edward's preconceptions and repression gets challenged by a beautiful and highly sexual work colleague. Shona's efforts to provoke her boyfriend Dan prove too successful. *On Blindness* incorporated sign language and audio description.

UK tour

Commissioned by the Brighton International Festival
Written by Michael Wynne
Directed by Scott Graham and Steven Hoggett
Choreography by Scott Graham and Steven Hoggett and the company
Design by Dick Bird
Lighting design by Natasha Chivers
Music by Goldfrapp
Assistant Director: Neil Bettles

Cast: Cait Davis, Delphine Gaborit, Ian Golding, Georgina Lamb, Eddie Kay, Imogen Knight, David Sibley, Liam Steel, Joseph Traynor (plus 20 performance students from the BRIT School, Croydon)

A unique guided tour of excess through the ballrooms and bedrooms of a Brighton hotel. The hotel is closing down and Alex is being treated to a dirty weekend by his girlfriend. As soon as they check in he loses her and his search takes him through the rotten underbelly beneath the fading chic of this once glamorous seafront hotel.

Brighton International Festival

A Frantic Assembly, Drum Theatre Plymouth and Lyric Hammersmith
    production
Written by Mark Ravenhill
Directed and choreographed by Scott Graham and Steven Hoggett
Design by Miriam Beuther
Lighting design by Natasha Chivers

Cast: Keir Charles, Cait Davis, Leah Muller, Mark Rice-Oxley

After a horrific accident where she jumps into an empty swimming pool, a
famous artist convalesces under the protection of her four oldest friends. Soon
their care turns to bitterness and her suffering becomes their next work of art.

*UK Tour, nominated for TMA award – Best Touring Production and winner of
the Peter Wolff Theatre Trust supports The Whiting Award 2008*

Frantic Assembly and Drum Theatre Plymouth production
Written by Bryony Lavery
Directed and choreographed by Scott Graham and Steven Hoggett
Design by Laura Hopkins
Lighting design by Andy Purves
Sound design by Adrienne Quartly

Cast: Samuel James, Georgina Lamb

Todd and Kali love each other to bits. They have the perfect life. *Stockholm*
delves into a world of obsessive love and its brutal consequences.

UK Tour

Frantic Assembly and Theatre Royal Plymouth in collaboration with Royal
    and Derngate Northampton
Adapted and directed by Scott Graham and Steven Hoggett
Design by Laura Hopkins

Lighting design by Natasha Chivers
Sound design by Gareth Fry
Assistant Director: Jamie Rocha Allan
Soundtrack by Hybrid
Choreographed by Scott Graham, Steven Hoggett and the company

Cast: Charles Aitken, Jimmy Akingbola, Claire-Louise Cordwell, Leila Crerar, Minnie Crowe, Marshall Griffin, Richard James-Neale, Eddie Kay, Jami Reid-Quarrell

Set in a pub at the heart of the growing racial tension in West Yorkshire in 2001.

UK Tour

Additional work

Below are details of other productions where we have been involved in the movement direction, co-direction or choreography.

(As Frantic Assembly)

Vs	Cairo International Festival
Improper	Bare Bones Dance Company
Market Boy	National Theatre, dir. Rufus Norris
Villette	Stephen Joseph Theatre, dir. Laurie Sansom
Frankenstein	Northampton Royal & Derngate Theatres, dir. Laurie Sansom
The Hot House	National Theatre, dir. Ian Rickson
The May Queen	Everyman Theatre, dir. Serdar Bilis
On the Rocks	Hampstead Theatre, dir. Clare Lizzimore

(Separately – a selection)

Mercury Fur	Paines Plough, dir. John Tiffany
Home (Inverness)	National Theatre of Scotland
Black Watch	National Theatre of Scotland, dir. John Tiffany
The Bacchae	National Theatre of Scotland, dir. John Tiffany
365	National Theatre of Scotland, dir. Vicky Featherstone

Othello, 2008 © Manuel Harlan

part one

documentation

chapter one

Frantic essays

Here are some thoughts that might give you an insight into our creative process. We also attempt to answer some of the more frequently asked questions about our company, our work and our working relationship.

Pre-show

From the very start there was the notion of the pre-show. For us, these were those unique minutes between entering the performance space and the start of the performance proper. These minutes are there for the taking – a time when the level of expectation is palpable and yet malleable, a time that naturally fuels slightly animated conversation; and yet even this very personal factor can be manipulated.

The drive behind the pre-show had a lot to do with being a company about to set out on a multi-venue tour for the first time. In creating a pre-show we felt we achieved two vital factors. One was the claiming of the space. From the moment each audience member entered the auditorium, they were instantly made aware that the space was ours, had been claimed by Frantic. No matter that they were long-serving season ticket holders, used to swinging through those same doors twice a month. Our aim was not necessarily to wrong-foot them – in most cases this was never going to be possible with a couple of bits of Tri-Lite and a swathe of MDF (i.e. our set). The ambition was to stake out our territorial claim, that in some way tonight might be different from what they might usually expect, that things were in our control for tonight. During those early tours, venues changed dramatically from town to town and night to night. Wings suddenly disappeared or were only found on one side. The audience were on top of us one night and then were somewhere out there in the darkness the next. The speaker systems were right behind us, kicking out decibels that created involuntary movement among us, or consisted of a tiny speaker somewhere up in the lighting rig and in front of us so that we were effectively performing in silence on stage. Such oscillations in stage experiences were par for the course once the show began so it was always a relief to feel that those starting minutes would be something we could set off with, collectively. A few precious moments of control before the technical capacity of the venue and the responses of the audience that night started to have their own effect.

The pre-shows varied from piece to piece but the underlying principle was (and still is) to create the idea that something *has already started*. That the price of your ticket wasn't enough to contain the start of the work, that this was a place where you would be asked to keep up, a place where the stuffy conventions of polite chatter were not an option.

For our very first pre-show (*Look Back in Anger*) we gauged a moment when we figured approximately 50 percent of the audience had taken their seats. At this point, there was a 30-second blast from a Nine Inch Nails track (famed American Industrial/Techno/Grunge artist Trent Reznor) during which we emerged from both wings (when available) and executed a furious blast of movement upon each other, at the end of which we disappeared until the start of the show when the entire audience were in. A sort of 'blink and you miss it' sequence or 'miss it completely 'cos you were still getting your ticket ripped' sequence. Whichever, it got the seated audience wired and created a great 'we saw this weird beginning thing/what are you talking about?' divide in the bar afterwards.

From there, pre-shows have ranged from blasting the audience with pounding techno music as they enter (*Klub*), the entire cast being concealed within a toilet cubicle on stage while a soundtrack relays the recorded events of an alcohol-fuelled evening together (*Sell Out*) and the performers casually chatting while suspended as high as the venue would allow from four separate golden ladders (*Hymns*). Our personal favourite was the pre-show for *Flesh* which we based on an account given to us in interview by a male prostitute during our research for the show. He described how he would pick up clients on street corners by 'jigging around a bit'. From this we created a start to the show where the four performers would prowl the stage as the audience entered, eyeing them up and staring at various people, intermittently dropping into various 'jigs' as a means of flirtation. The collective task was to 'find your person'. At the same time, we considered ourselves as something definitely not sexy but something closer to 'butcher's cuts'. The biggest crowd pleaser seemed to be the run-up to the opening of *Zero*. Five performers squeezed into an impossibly small children's Wendy house for sometimes up to twenty-five minutes as an unsuspecting (and as it sometimes felt, uncaring) audience sauntered in. Once the show properly began, the house began to pulse as the performers pressed into the little plastic walls before all bursting from the doors and windows, trying desperately not to show the extent of chronic cramp and pins and needles.

Some pre-shows did cause confusion for some audiences. A second pre-show for *Look Back in Anger* involved the performers on stage rehearsing the show for themselves quietly as the audience began to arrive, with a music track playing in the foreground. A rather elderly audience in Croydon, unable to hear what we were saying, began to yell at us furiously, telling us that they couldn't hear us, that we would have to speak up, that we had to have the music turned down.

Even at its most basic, the pre-show was a carefully selected music track played at a volume level that forced the incoming audience to shout slightly if they wished to talk to one another once they were seated. An attempt to raise the adrenalin and create an underlying level of *event*.

As with all things, there were exceptions and mistakes. The pre-show for *Tiny Dynamite* was a bare stage with the gentle sound of crickets, easily drowned out by audience chatter. The piece was a break from many practices for both Frantic and Paines Plough and to experiment in this way felt totally in keeping with the project as a whole. An initial pre-show for *Klub* involved the use of mid-level classical music which we felt was a trick that the audience could see through immediately. The first night that we swapped Schubert for The Aloof at top levels, the audience cheered as the lights went down before a single thing had happened on stage.

For us, the pre-show is a precious device, not in the sense of being delicate or even necessarily well crafted (though we did spend weeks working on the pre-show for *Flesh*), but precious as in valuable, an essential part of what we perceive to be the theatrical experience of coming to see a Frantic show. Laying claim to a theatre space like this demonstrates that we are taking full responsibility for what is about to happen and in fact, it is already happening. It creates a sense of event by asking the audience to commit to the experience just that little bit earlier than they might usually expect, to give just that little bit more. It is this kind of contract that Frantic wishes to engage in and to provide.

Truth and lies – persona and performance

During the summer of 1995 while devising *Klub*, we had a discussion about what our character names might be. The session swiftly degenerated into idiocy and a unanimous inability to take the task seriously. Without the particulars of period or setting, the task itself seemed irrelevant in relation to the piece. With any name seeming as good as any other, the decision between Callum or Cleetus became insurmountable to us. An initial idea for us to assume our own names was deemed too confusing at the time as there were two performers in the company with the same name, Korina Biggs and Karina Sarmiento. However, with all other attempts proving futile, our script writer and performer, Spencer, started to use our names in the scripts that he was handing in at the beginning of rehearsals.

The immediate effect this had was both primitive and electrifying. During first readings of the scenes we found that hearing our own names created an innate emotional reflex, adding an incredible energy to the scenes. Our names come with so much history and our lifetimes are littered with experiences and memories where we have heard our own names uttered, whispered, yelled, screamed, sung, etc. It seems obvious now, but at the time we had no idea of the power behind hearing your own name within a performance – the shocking sense of 'nowness' that it creates, its ability to knock you out of the most fuggy actorly daze. There seemed to be such an intrinsic honesty about this device that matched our attempt to create stage text taken from our own life experience.

As with any discovery, we soon became aware of the limitations and problems too. Overuse of our names soon sounded like the introductory session of a self-help group. It had already been decided that the bulk of the text in *Klub* would be delivered as direct address (after experimenting with this form in our previous production of *Look Back in Anger*) and again, this provided its own problems. When referring to each other by name to the audience, it sometimes felt as if we were 'announcing' each other rather than simply referring to one another. All these discoveries were vital in setting out the 'rules' for the convention (a convention we were to continue using extensively for the next four years – it becoming something of a signature device for Frantic performers on stage).

Referring to one another *as* one another also had repercussions elsewhere. The choice not to afford ourselves another 'name' seemed only to ring true by not affording ourselves some other 'voice'. The challenge then (and it was a challenge) was to ensure that, at any given moment, the delivery of lines was as natural as we could possibly make it. As a company, we took on board the responsibility of 'busting' one another if anything sounded out of the ordinary from any one individual. With most of us having undergone no formal acting or performance training we seemed to be floundering in the dark and certainly the performances in our first production, *Look Back in Anger*, contained some rather strange interpretations of Received Pronunciation (RP). It is possible that our lack of training, coupled with a very limited experience of theatre as audience members, meant that we were somewhat beholden to a style of theatrical speech. It was no small relief during *Klub* when we allowed ourselves to speak to the audience as we might in the bar afterwards. 'Busting' one another also became fascinating when we started to note how company members would unwittingly start to adopt inflections and characteristics from other company members, accidental imitations. Korina, middle-class Norwich born and bred, had started to sneak in a subtle flattening of the vowels on occasion and Steven's Yorkshire roots wrapped themselves in frustration one day around the word 'plaster'. So without any set or formal training it seemed that we had to go through a period of 'unlearning' in order to find the vocal delivery style that was only ever our own in the first place.

Each show within the 'Generation Trilogy' (*Klub*, *Flesh* and *Zero*) used the very simple device of a downstage spotlit microphone from which the performers would use direct address in communicating with the audience. From this position (and anywhere else on stage) we were careful to avoid what we called the 'ether effect' (also known as the 'dancer's gaze'). This ongoing practice seems to infiltrate many productions, both theatre and dance, and is, by definition, the moment at which the performer, on facing the audience, suddenly finds a point, usually between 12 and 20 inches above the audience. On finding this point, the performer then adopts a glazed expression that they continue to hold throughout the movement section or speech. It is usually coupled with a general countenance of awe and/or reverie. We always felt that it suggested some supreme smugness and an almost cowardly reluctance to engage with the paying public sat within spitting distance. The flip-side of this, and no less troublesome, is the 'In Yer Face' glare. Again, a very popular choice, particularly among physical theatre companies. This involves practically glowering at the audience beyond the point of it seeming like a challenging moment and more like an invitation to take it outside. You have only to be on the end of this once to know that it is only in very rare moments that this method actually does what it should. We were meticulous in detailing for ourselves a way to quite simply 'talk' to the audience, to 'see' them rather than be seen 'looking' at them. We were obsessive about the idea of 'being' rather than necessarily 'communicating'. The latter is something we are much better at now, but at the time, achieving this state seemed to send us down some very peculiar paths of practice.

The use of our own names coupled with this distinct off-the-cuff vocal delivery (a smorgasbord of regional and international accents), usually detailing incredibly personal stories, meant that the effect on the audience often gave rise to some very interesting responses on their part regarding notions of 'honesty'. Over the three shows there were consistencies of character within the stories and accounts. (In rehearsals it didn't always follow that we kept our own stories – the final result usually saw our onstage personae being a mish-mash of pure fiction and the company's collective individual experiences.) The commitment to this confessional sincerity reached its fruition during the *Zero* tour when it became apparent that people really had believed that everything we had said over the last three years was absolutely true of ourselves. Post-show discussions and bar conversations saw Cait Davis being bombarded with questions about her kid (*Zero*), her sex-for-cash exploits during college (*Flesh*) and her ex-boyfriend Doug (*Klub*). It was surprising the number of people who genuinely seemed quite annoyed that we had 'lied' to them and no end of pointing out the basic tenets of theatre was going to appease them. Such protests made us exceedingly happy. It seemed to be a fine line between truly engaging with your audience and duping them, but it is one we were very happy to tread.

Accidents and creativity

The Frantic rehearsal room is a well-considered space but not always the most organised. There will always be a source of sugar somewhere in the room and a good-sized pair of speakers to contend with, but the actual plan for the day falls well short of a military-type strategy with hours mapped out and scenes to be ticked off. One of the occasional pitfalls of sharing the directorial respon-sibility is believing that you can ignore a scene or section that feels tricky to initiate or start, hoping that the other will pick it up and run. The problem in our case is that we always have the same reluctance about the exact same scenes. The physical element in our work means that there is quite a methodical approach to the physical side of rehearsals but we are long-term advocates of a slightly looser approach to theatre making when it comes to creating and developing scenes. This is partly because of the many fortuitous moments that have occurred in rehearsals by way of keeping an eye on everything that is happening in the room. This means allowing even the most random event to shape and alter an exercise, to leave the path or idea prescribed maybe only moments earlier and to free up the room in order to make the most of a newfound impulse, influence or inclination. We have always maintained that on day one of rehearsals, the notebooks we carry into the rehearsal room will be of the highest quality (we spend weeks on the search for working notebooks that satisfy all the requisite standards) but will not contain all the answers. They are there for us to map out the gradual process of how each show comes into being, not ticking off pre-decided scenes and sequences already mapped out.

An early example of this was on our first day of rehearsals for *Zero* which was a devised performance working around the idea of pre-millennial tension coming to a climax during a house party on New Year's Eve 1999. We had strong reservations about a set that represented the inside of a house. All pre-rehearsal conversations regarding the look and feel of the house and its room or rooms proved fruitless. This was at a time when there was no designer employed on our productions, and in this instance we strongly felt the lack of that individual who provides expert input on aesthetic issues, practicality and possibility. On entering the sports hall of the Welsh girls' school that was to be our home for the next five weeks, we were met by a slightly embarrassed looking children's Wendy house into which we all promptly disappeared for the next hour (the five of us all being under the national average height was, in this instance, a blessing, meaning we could just fit in en masse). Our whole problem of the interior of the space, all the choices that would have to go into the presentation of our playing environment, was erased as we realised the answer lay in this tatty plastic house that stood approximately four feet high. Our capacity to present a party going on inside this tiny house was priceless – allowing us to flip between riotous action by the house itself and then scenes of personal, private introspection practically anywhere else on stage by virtue of it being outside the house. Our entire playing space freed itself up to many possibilities, and the capacity for the house party to be the best of all possible parties was unquestioned, it only being glimpsed every now and again through the tiny windows and door. The fact that so many people wanted to be in such a small space went some way to representing the desirability for all the characters to be at the party, even though in real terms it often meant much discomfort for the performers and some very intimate physical encounters in there – some expected, some not.

Another example occurred during rehearsals for *Hymns* and an early impro-visation for a scene we finally called Lullaby. At the time, we were improvising a scene around a table between the four characters using the simple practice of physically 'listening' to one another and attempting to construct a sequence using physical impulses taken from each other. As a character objective, we didn't want to be seen communicating anything too committed but at the same time yearned for just the simplest form of connection that remained elusive. We ran a number of sessions attempting to set this sequence, each time working with a track by the band lamb that was the final track on their album *Fear of Fours*. It was felt that the rhythm contained in the track drove the urgency of the exercise in a way that was useful in conveying a sense of insistence, of wanting to connect. During a late run of the exercise, as the track finished, nobody pressed stop on the CD player. Unusually for us, the exercise continued in silence after the track had completed. What we didn't realise was that lamb had a tendency to include 'hidden' tracks on their CDs – a track that plays some time after the ending of the last listed track. In this case it was some time before the track 'Lullaby' quietly drifted out of the speakers. At first, no-one really knew what was happening but what became apparent was that this was a whole new mood and tempo being offered. The exercise switched, becoming something far more delicate. The rhythms slowed and the painful misses in trying to connect with one another came to the fore. Playing to the music, we totally rediscovered the scene for ourselves and less than three minutes later we had what was very close to the completed version of our scene. This was one of the first rehearsal periods where we had use of a video camera and it is this 'Lullaby' episode that we often cite as the turning point for us in the way that we record and create work in the rehearsal room.

A second 'happy accident' occurred during the making of Lullaby a few weeks later when we moved to a rehearsal studio at Battersea Arts Centre, which had a huge window at one side. As we were running and recording the sequence, a sudden dramatic flurry of clouds scudded across the sky outside, breaking up the sun's rays and sending long shadows shifting across the table at which we were all sat. The sudden speed of the light moving around the room looked like time-lapse photography. Luckily, the video recording was as dramatic looking as the actual event and we were able to hand the tape over to Natasha Chivers, our lighting designer, who replicated the sequence of light for the actual show.

While dance companies gravitate to light and airy rooms with polished mirrors we have found that the slightly more down-market rooms have actually had more impact on the rehearsals. When rehearsing *Hymns* we spent the first three weeks in an extremely plush dance studio in a new purpose-built venue. And we found it less than perfect. The beautiful, clean lines may have been conducive to pure dance and to be fair we did work very hard creating a large proportion of the more dancy elements of the show, but we struggled to get any theatrical inspiration. A case of all perspiration and no inspiration. We were in danger of leaving that space still unsure about ideas surrounding set and design. We knew we wanted ladders but how could we tour with them? How could we slide down them like we imagined without shredding our hands? What was the overall aesthetic of the piece? It was when we were looking through a maintenance cupboard for a mop to clean up a spill on the immaculate sprung floor that we found a ladder. The sides were smooth and it broke down into 90 centimeter sections which meant we could potentially create the 5 metre ladders we hoped for and still be able to tour with it. We contacted the manufacturer and they sent us our ladder pieces. This accidental discovery was probably the most important moment of our three weeks rehearsing at a premiere dance studio.

Accidents that have befallen our actors have made it into final productions. During a late rehearsal for *Rabbit*, one section involved the actress Sue Kyd suddenly turning on her daughter and marching across the room towards her. On this occasion, as Sue rounded the set and set off on her trajectory, her heel collapsed and rather than stopping, she carried on her path, but in this instance her march had turned into a lurch as Sue tried to navigate the constantly shifting balance of her walking pattern, rising and falling like a careering, stunned animal about to crash to the ground. The effect was startling and encapsulated the moment so precisely that, in the final production, we not only had her repeat the event, but also armed her with a bottle of vodka in each hand just to add to the swagger of the moment.

Examples such as these are less about pre-thought ideas proving to be wrong and more about the essential practice of being truly receptive to ideas and influences that occur around the rehearsal period. It is not unknown for us to work on an image that one of us might have spotted on an advertising billboard on the way into work that morning. The set for *Tiny Dynamite* was a direct reference to the series of *Big Brother* that we were all watching on TV that summer. The show's title was a pure mistake, taken from a song by Cocteau Twins that is actually called 'Tiny Dynamine'. It is important to remember that happy accidents can never be relied on. Nothing is more terrifying for us than the notion of turning up in a room and just 'seeing what happens', but what we have also discovered is that if the rehearsal process is structured and ordered to the point of being sanitised, then you don't allow the space for these happy accidents to happen.

What is physical theatre? (and why we hate answering that question)

We get asked this a lot. We always try to answer to the best of our abilities but therein lies the problem. Each time we answer we feel that the person asking the question actually knows more about the subject than we do.

This is not a question that occupies much of our time, despite the number of times we get asked it. 'Physical theatre' is actually quite a frustrating phrase as it barely manages to describe what we do never mind the wide range of styles and influences that are clustered under its banner.

When we have tried to avoid the question it is only partly through boredom and mostly through ignorance. We will do our best now to explain what it means to us but that won't be easy. We do not come from a formal theatre background and have not been instructed in the history of performance. We are not particularly familiar with terms and definitions that are often contained within the questions addressed to us. Once, in front of a class of theatre undergraduates, when asked to talk about how Artaud had influenced us, we started to rattle off venue names, how each audience was different and the joys of sleeping in a Transit van. We thought they wanted to know about our tour. This was not just a case of mishearing. The students were horrified to find that we had never heard of Artaud. In fact there was honesty and relevance in our accidental answer. The Transit van we used to tour actually did have much more influence over our work than any practitioner in a textbook.

It appears 'physical theatre' is used as an umbrella term for aspects of performance including dance theatre, mime, clowning and traditional pictorial or visual theatre. (We are already way out of our comfort zone!) Within this is an enormous range of 'physicality' from the limb-threateningly expressive to the delicate and demonstrative. It can be said that our brand of theatre sits somewhere within this realm and could rightly be termed physical theatre.

When we started our company we were proud and excited to be labelled under the physical theatre banner. We were fit and fearless and just wanted to bang the drum for the physical theatre cause.

As we developed and the questions about physical theatre mounted up we started to realise that it was not particularly applicable to our creative process. The question 'What is physical theatre?' only crossed our mind replying to e-mails from students. We were not interested in definitions as, to us, they felt like limitations. Our unorthodox route into theatre had actually presented us with a world of possible styles and approaches. We realised quickly that this was our strength. We were not developed through a house style as can happen at some establishments. We were not dedicated to exploring theatre through Brechtian terms. The world was our oyster.

It is true to say that we set out to be Volcano Theatre Company clones, such was their immediate influence on us, but that soon faded. We were not as politicised or as angry as Volcano. We had a lighter touch. Watching a Volcano show that we did not enjoy was possibly one of the most liberating experiences as it helped us find what we did like. This is a pattern that continued for many years, acting instinctively and finding out what we did like by noticing what we didn't. This experience did not dull our appreciation of Volcano. It just told us that we were not Volcano.

We became influenced by the dance films of DV8. Through attending workshops we encountered influential practitioners from dance companies such as V-TOL and the Featherstonehaughs. Even at this early stage we did not see distinctions between movement and theatre. It was all there to be harnessed. This was not, however, through a desire to be genre breaking. It was because we were not aware of definitions.

As we have developed we have become more aware of the dangers of existing under a banner. People expect you to deliver work along those lines. Being aware meant that we have openly reserved the right to make the kind of theatre we like. That was our reason for starting off and that must not change. When we made *Tiny Dynamite* we were desperate to remain true to its need for a gentle and tender physicality. It was still a physical show in our minds. It just had none of the bombast and spectacle of what one might expect from 'physical theatre'.

It is this expectation that frightens us. We do not want to simply deliver the expected.

Director/Director relationship

Frantic Assembly has two artistic directors. We have worked together through-out our professional career and people often ask if we agree on everything. The answer is simply no. If we did, there would be no need to have two directors. We would simply be saying the same thing twice.

When there is disagreement there is also a trust that allows one partner to run with their controversial idea and probably convince the other partner of its merits. If a partner is willing to fight for an idea, then there must be something of worth there. We have seen this enough times through the years to let it happen, knowing that the unconvinced partner will probably catch up soon enough and, no doubt, offer the finishing touches that the first partner may have been too involved to notice. The phrase 'you cross 'em over and I'll nod 'em in' has been heard more than once in the rehearsal room.

But that is after many years of working together, developing what can appear to be a shorthand bordering on telepathy. The important thing each of us had to learn was that a question about your idea is not simply a challenge. It is another opportunity for you to put it across, to clarify your intention. It is crucial to create a working environment of trust and support, where the airing of ideas does not feel like walking a tightrope while the locals throw fruit at you. When, individually, we felt that we were being challenged in the rehearsal room, we had to control that raging voice that suggests running to the hills, remember that theatre is about the transference of ideas, and try once again to see if our collaborators can see the merits of our idea. When they cannot there comes a point when you have to look around the room, remember that you are working with people you trust and respect, and that there must be some flaw in the idea for it to stumble at this early stage. It is better that the idea is tested and fails here than is allowed to run into the performance without the understanding and appreciation of your collaborators.

It is very important not to feel defeated at this point. If you trust your idea, then it will return stronger. You will find a better way to communicate it. All that your collaborators need is to be able to trust that idea too. That is when they will open up and join you on the task of putting this idea on stage. As they all usually come from different areas of expertise they can all usually offer a different angle of attack. Or even better they can appreciate that your angle, or someone else's, is the best.

There have been many times when one of us has had to play catch up to an idea that just would not die. The process of questions, even doubts, has made the idea stronger than ever. Once that idea comes back and we finally are on the same page then things start to fly. We can feel confident that we are understood, that we understand, and that we can offer something to the idea.

This has been a long process and one where we have often bitten our tongue and burned with anger, but it has given rise to the development of a trust that suggests 'I am not sure I fully appreciate this idea at the moment, but if I know you and you feel that this idea is right and worth sharing, then I will do my best to open my mind and catch up because I trust you.' Admittedly not much of a catch-phrase, but it does emphasise each of our positions in this partnership. We are the other's sounding board. We are the key to making this happen. We are the support. We are the missing link. We will make sense of it when it starts to ache our partner's head. We are the fiercest critic because it matters. So what we have in this partnership is that understanding. With that comes the need to surprise and challenge each other. One of us would not have a certain idea if it was not for direct or indirect inspiration from the other.

Scott Graham and Steven Hoggett, Director/Director: rehearsing *Othello*, 2008 © Manuel Harlan

This is also a collaborative, devising partnership that recognises the need to look outside itself frequently for inspiration. Just as we believe that the director does not posses all knowledge from within their black book, we accept that the creative output of Frantic Assembly could not purely come from within the world of its two artistic directors. Collaborating with so many brilliant people slowly teaches you something more than devising techniques and fancy shapes. It has taught us that if someone you trust and respect shares their idea with you, they do it for a reason. It is because they need to, because they want to and because they trust you. When you realise that, it raises your game.

Video camera in rehearsal

Our rehearsal rooms are now full of sound systems and people tapping away at laptops. It is a long way from the empty rooms and the vacant looks that accompanied our initial rehearsals. The technological revolution in the way we work has mostly crept up on us, but there was a moment when we took a great lurch forward. It was a time when the video camera became a necessity in the rehearsal room.

We started making *Heavenly* in January 2002. We were working with a close friend as fellow writers, directors, choreographers and performers. For

Jimmy Akingbola and Claire-Louise Cordwell in rehearsal for *Othello*, 2008 © Manuel Harlan

From rehearsal to production – Richard Winsor and Ifan Meredith as Monster and Victor Frankenstein. *Frankenstein*, 2008

most rehearsal sessions it was just the three of us trying to make work that was poignant and funny. For three people who could make each other laugh effortlessly we found the whole process of turning material into a show torturous. We were lost and alone and losing all confidence. We struck upon the idea of bringing in a video camera and setting up improvisations we could all take part in. We set the camera up and ran the exercise. When we had finished we rushed to the camera and rewound it knowing there were some good moments in there. Watching it back gave us a bit of a shock. All of the good bits were accidental; all of the bits we thought were good were anything but. This might have been a deflating experience had the camera not given us all of these moments we had missed. It was up to us now to gather them up and consciously put them into our work.

The video camera had saved us on that project. We made sure that we took it into subsequent productions, thinking that it is one thing for us to stand out front and tell performers where their improvisations were and were not working, and another to sit down with them and analyse what they were doing and the possibilities that emerge accidentally and get captured by the camera. The performers can then recreate those moments and claim them for their own.

The video camera is not just for capturing and documenting what you know is there. It is also for capturing all the possibilities that emerge by accident. It is there to show you what you don't yet know. It is also a great shorthand way of explaining to a performer what you liked and what you want them to do. Watching a recording of an improvisation enables you to specify moments by the minute and second they occurred. This means that performers can recreate the moments and move towards a final version that is an amalgamation of killer moves from longer improvisations. This process was invaluable on productions like *Frankenstein* (adapted by Lisa Evans), where the improvisations were so physically and mentally draining that the performers had no sense of what worked and what did not. This process allowed them to go straight to those moments, saving them from the exhaustion of repeating the improvisations.

Physical truth and characterisation

The concept of physical characterisation came late to Frantic Assembly. With the Generation Trilogy shows (*Klub*, *Flesh* and *Zero*) our notion of characterisation was minimal. In each of these, our work tended to focus on creating physical performances that were as close to our everyday physicality as possible. The shift started with *Sell Out*, where the writer Michael Wynne wrenched us from our comfort zone by intentionally misspelling all our real names in the script, but it was with the following show, *Hymns*, that we really began to tackle the idea of creating a physical character.

The process itself is understood and used widely in traditional theatre making, though our own experience is that it is often a process that proves, at best, typical in its results and, at worst, a waste of a morning. The 'physical characterisation' session usually takes place in the first week of a rehearsal period and will involve the actors knowing little or nothing about their characters. The session is often used as the means by which the actors might begin to understand their character. After many years working with some truly gifted physical performers, we have yet to be convinced that a single session at this stage does much for anybody's understanding of their character. Using physicality is rarely a short cut for anything – as the rehearsal schedule for a physical theatre piece or dance theatre performance will attest to. There should be no distinction drawn between the ways that an actor might understand their character by way of textual analysis and physical analysis and experimentation. Like the ways in which a scene from a production is returned to in order to consolidate, develop and progress, the ongoing development of physical characterisation must be mapped out along the entire timeline of any rehearsal schedule. Physical discoveries made in an initial session cannot possibly hold true given the momentous shifts and discoveries that occur during even the most predictable or well-planned rehearsal period.

As well as providing the time and space for physical characterisation, the actor must also be provided with directorial support. It is surprising how many totally competent directors will seemingly shy away from noting an actor in reference to their physicality on stage and in the rehearsal room. In our experience, actors have less difficulty being noted on their physicality than any other part of their performance and in most cases relish the fact that they are being considered and observed in this way. This belief holds true not just for Frantic rehearsals. Most actors, given the correct support network, have a fantastic capacity for experimentation with their physicality. This might be in the creation of particular traits for a specific character but is also true in searching for physical 'truths'. Some of the most enjoyable sessions in our careers have been spent finding the physical truth behind an epileptic fit or the impact of a snowball.

Any work undertaken by us in this area is a healthy combination of searching for both physical characterisations and physical truths. Different productions have required very different approaches to physicality in these respects. It is rare that we would run a session where the performers would be asked to walk around the space using their everyday physicality and then, in considering their given character, attempt to discover their 'walk'. This exercise asks too much too soon for the results to be genuinely useful and these results are often rooted in stereotype and cliché. Working with Laurie Sansom for the first

Physical characterisation: Georgina Lamb in *Villette*, 2005

time on *Villette* we discovered that a simple way to avoid the regular pitfalls of this type of work is to create a follow-up session soon after any initial work has been done in finding a character's physicality. The session falls into two distinct categories – development and challenges. It is important that the term 'challenge' is used in the correct way here – an opportunity to be taken up rather than a correction of something that is wrong or failing.

To help develop the range and understanding of any physical decisions that have been made, ask the actors to place themselves in a comfortable, relaxed position – sitting is normally a good idea. You might want to give them a simple object or activity, but this should be just that – simple. Having a magazine in your hand is useful; reading it less so. From here, ask the group to recall their discoveries and play out their newfound physical character. This level is perhaps best referred to as 'at rest' – where the actor is actively involved in creating physical characterisation but at a point when the actual character is themselves in a state of relaxation, neutrality, calm. In order to play the sub-tleties of their discoveries, the group should then be asked to discover and explore this same set of choices but this time imagining a circumstance where the character is experiencing difficulty being their regular self physically and has to exert extra effort in order to achieve neutrality. Such an example might be where the character is tired, bored, distracted or drunk. The other end of this exercise is for the group to explore their physicality as this character in an imagined scenario where the opposite is true, where they feel they have to suppress their physicality. Examples might be having to withhold information or restraining themselves from expressing physical or verbal violence.

Simple challenges can go a long way towards preventing actors falling into either cliché or personal physical habits. One such challenge would be to ask the group to look at left and right choices that they have made with their physicality. For instance, if the physical characterisation involves the choice of the left shoulder being slightly rounded and raised, ask the actor to switch this to the other side. In most creative choices, we still conform to the natural impulses and construct of our bodies and it can take an outside challenge to reverse these impulses before we physically create something genuinely new to ourselves. Another challenge might be to ask members of the group to trade a particular physical characteristic with one another. This is best done at an early stage but can again be a great way of breaking habitual practice. Asking an actor to transfer an upper body physical character choice to their lower half (or vice versa) might not always be a successful experiment but it might be a useful one. With both these exercises, allow thinking time and in this way look to avoid easy, typical practice.

Another important factor to consider is the physical character in relation to the environment. We found this for ourselves during the rehearsals for *Rabbit*, where we were fortunate enough to have the set in rehearsals from a very early stage. (The advantages of this were so great that this is now a requisite for any Frantic rehearsal process.) During the first week of rehearsals we had covered some ground on character through textual analysis of the play but nothing too detailed. At this point the performers were little more than an upper-middle-class couple, their long-suffering chauffeur, their frustrated daughter and her heroin addict boyfriend. As a way into their characterisation we ran two considerably lengthy improvisation sessions. The first one was in response to the set as a structural entity. Dick Bird designed the interior of a super-modern holiday home in the middle of a forest, all brilliant white space-age minimalist furniture and expansive windows looking out onto forests and mountains, its sparse interior designed to within an inch of its life in total contrast with the lush, colour-drenched, naturally splendorous view it overlooked. At first individually, the actors were asked to explore the set in terms of where to simply 'be'; to find where they might sit or stand in different circumstances – in order to feel safe perhaps or in order to be able to make a quick getaway; where they might want to be in relation to the expansive view outside; whether the curve of the windowsill was something they considered pleasurable and full of movement to explore or whether it instilled a careering sense of instability. A second run of this exercise involved various combinations of the characters in the room at the same time. They were all asked to consider whether the sudden presence of one of the other characters changed their perception and use of the same space and to then play out that newfound mode of physical operation.

The second exercise to follow on from this involved the input of props into the set. As the family's holiday home, the set contained a few objects, most of them involving the expansive bar and drinks-making facilities enjoyed by the family. There was also an as yet still alive rabbit that was due to form the centrepiece of that night's dining table. In order to facilitate the exercise we also threw in a few extra objects such as magazines and coffee table type books. The performers then ran the same exercise of discovery, but this time in terms of the literal contents of the room – at first one by one and then in various combinations.

By filming these sessions on the video camera we provided ourselves with a wealth of information that we used constantly throughout the entire rehearsal period. Physical patterns, traits and responses were noted by the company and developed over the next five weeks. (It is important to note that these were taken as starting points, not as end points.) Observing the literal walking patterns of the actors allowed us to create the entire physical structure of a very dense textual scene in the play. An instruction to be dynamic within the space during the second attempt of the exercise gave rise to a whole new vocabulary of athleticism, risk taking and daring within the space that then became the source of a physical solo we developed for the chauffeur. This included heightened and ballistic movement that stemmed from simple activities such as sitting down, moving from the floor to the window ledge and reaching for a bottle or champagne glass.

Working at this second level is important in producing the more dynamic physical moments and material for a Frantic show. However, it is very much a second level and must always be preceded by an initial level that looks for something far more truthful. By truthful we mean discovering physical language that is totally natural, unexceptional and yet incredibly considered – a physical sense of character that does not include limps, twitches, spasms and other easy, flashy, scene-stealing tics. Discovering physical truth is always an extraordinary journey. Often it upturns received wisdom about how we are as physical beings. During preparations for *Tiny Dynamite*, Vicky Featherstone asked us all to close our eyes and simulate walking through an unknown room. Instinctively we all began to use our arms to create wide, sweeping arm patterns. Locking yourself in a truly pitch-black room and attempting the same reveals the physical truth that we are more prone to pat the air around us than make the free sweeping gestures we imagine we employ in such a scenario.

If you were to research the work of Frantic through the critical response to our productions, much is made of the limb-threatening, high-octane, full-blown physicality that has become our trademark. Though this end of the physical spectrum is one that we are happy to call our home, we are as dedicated, if

David Sibley, *Dirty Wonderland*, 2005

THE FRANTIC ASSEMBLY BOOK OF DEVISING THEATRE

not more so, to the subtle, nuanced end of the physical spectrum. Some of our most accomplished moments have been these tiny physical details. In creating precise moments of physical storytelling we truly earn the right to put physicality up there with text as a credible means of communicating with our audience.

Insecurity, pragmatism, and admitting you were wrong!

Sometimes good ideas come quickly. Some days you find yourself skipping home from rehearsal thinking you have cracked it. You have found the elixir. You *know* this is how the show should be done. This kind of conviction can be fantastic but it can also cloud your judgement. There have been times when we have absolutely thought that we have found the only way to do a scene or stumbled upon the most brilliant physical scene that encapsulates and lifts the whole production. Invariably our passions become dimmed. The love affair is over and we can see clearly now. The scene is not going to work.

Below are extracts from one of our rehearsal diaries from *pool (no water)* by Mark Ravenhill. They touch on the journey of a scene we had absolute faith and conviction in. We had worked on it in the research and development sessions and were convinced it was the overriding aesthetic of our show . . .

Day 7

We started them off on an exercise to find ten fairly naturalistic sitting postures or moves while sat. They were to then set, remember these and turn them into a string of material. This is to be clearly defined and disciplined and possible, keeping to the count of the music used. This is only to create a vocabulary, though, and a sense of disciplined movement. There is not necessarily an intention to use the movement in this way in the production. This is so that we can use a precise physical language underneath the opening sections of text. Physicality that can unite the characters while we are making every effort to separate them textually and vocally. It can suggest complicity and insincerity or awkwardness. It immediately can present a conflict between what the characters say and what they mean and this instantly makes them more interesting. This exercise proves tough for some but the results are uniformly good.

We try out a different exercise for the first time. We set up a camera in a small room and instruct the performers to enter one at a time and be interviewed. We also tell them that they are allowed to play and choose different levels of excitement about this interview. But what we subject them to is the pre-interview and during this we witness the constant adjustments of chairs, clothes for lighting levels, sound checks and strange questions. All the time the camera is recording them, closing in and panning out.

We watch the recordings and it becomes fascinating how edgy they are and how difficult it is to achieve stillness when they have been knocked off guard by this strange situation. They display tiny twitches and insecurities, all written large on the TV screen. There is an unpredictable energy about the room and about these people. When later we attempt a semi-staged (seated) run-through of the first page the pace reaches a new low and that is when we refer the performers back to the video. That is what it was for – to combat this laid back, lazy, theatre raconteur delivery impulse that is afflicting us at the moment. We remind the performers that it is highly possible that the characters are not entirely at ease with the situation and it is this nervous energy that propels them on past tact and towards recklessness. Maybe they are disarmed by this situation.

Day 8

The rest of the afternoon is taken up with the performers all learning each other's ten moves in the chair from yesterday. They are very fast at this, despite being tired and sore. Their speed and clarity allows us to workshop the moves a little.

Day 9

Today has been quite a demanding day. We have been going through the text of the opening scene and choreographing each gesture and adjustment of each character sitting in their chair. This is painstaking, meticulous work and there are moments when the performers' brains appear to melt. It must be very hard and frustrating to persevere with this process without a clear idea of the overall effect. At first the performers appear to resist, to maintain and fight for their own naturalism and timing. Our job is to convince them of the artistic intention and how that requires a precision that will command and control the viewer's focus. But our job is also to remind the performer that they still have a role to play and skills to offer. They can easily feel like our puppets here, but once this choreography (for that is what it is and when this is understood, everything is easier) becomes second nature and embedded in a deep physical memory then the details the performers want to offer can emerge.

Day 19

(One of the performers had to take about a week off for family reasons.) After recapping and fitting him into some of what he has missed we start the run-through in front of the production team. Once again it starts off turgid, theatrical and just plain wrong. But this run is for memory, so slow is OK. And as far as that goes they were brilliant. But it is the directors that struggle . . .

The run does offer clarity though. It has to fizz along at a cracking pace. The characters have a story to tell and they want us to know but more importantly they need us to understand and that is where the energy comes from. That is the imperative. They could easily keep this story secret so they must have a need to tell it. They must also never take our understanding for granted. They must earn it and they must work harder when they sense that we are backing off from them.

Day 29 (first preview)

I suppose the show goes very well. It is hard to say because I cannot stand first nights and press nights. I just want to hide as I am not ready to discuss the show. People want to give me support and congratulations but I am just not capable of engaging. I have to apologise several times as I am sure it just appears rude and as if I do not believe the words of well-wishers. It is an unattractive trait we both share.

When we relax we are able to talk about the show with Simon Stokes, the artistic director of Plymouth Theatre Royal, and he offers confidence-building words and also constructive advice. And he is right. It was clear that we have to make some big but simple changes. There is a section at the start of the show where we had choreographed the awkward moves and adjustments of the characters and, to be honest, the performers never really pulled it off; but the reason why it has to go is because of Simon's specific observation – it is old style Frantic. It looked out of place in a show that is clearly a big step forward.

This will be easy to resolve. The scene was slower and more turgid than ever and meant the show had to work really hard to get through the gears.

It eventually got there but I spent the first 15 minutes begging them to speed up.

Day 30 (second preview)

We start the session with a speed line run in situ of the first scene and it is perfectly clear how liberating this is without the moves. I had always hated this scene as I thought that it was being strangled by the performers. Now I can see that it could have been us strangling them. They fly through the scene but it strikes me that this 'speed run' is not far from the pace I think it requires in performance. I tell the performers this and ask them to look out for and resist slipping into old habits with this scene.

. . .

We learnt our lesson here through the luxury of having a preview. We still sat through a really turgid performance with a paying public but at least it was advertised as a preview (if that really makes a difference in the eyes of the paying public).

This was a mistake we made despite all our talk of testing our work and remaining objective. Our stubbornness bordered on arrogance and we almost paid the price. What saved us was a structure that allowed us to look and think again (the previews) and the comments of a trusted friend (Artistic Director of Plymouth Theatre Royal, Simon Stokes).

We have, in the past, hidden from other people's comments after a show. Not through arrogance but fear. Now we do our best to listen and make ourselves available for feedback. More importantly, in rehearsals we have learnt to never become too fixed on an idea and to look at a problem in several ways before diagnosing it.

Frantic music and the notion of soundtracking

Throughout the development of Frantic Assembly, one of the most invigorating and exciting artistic discoveries has been that afforded by the exploration of music in our work. As a form, it has been the most essential of influences, not just in terms of creating the soundtracks for our shows but as a tool for setting up the right rehearsal environment, inspiring theatrical scenarios, offering inspiration through lyrical and compositional content, providing structure for improvisation sessions right through to the tracks used to accompany promotional material created by the company.

When facing the challenge of our first purely devised performance, *Klub*, we were liberated from all the constricts of a well-structured play, but with so much freedom at our disposal we were floundering in the vast sea of possibilities. Around this time we were starting to work with Andy Cleeton, a DJ also based in Swansea, which enjoyed a thriving club scene at the time. After hearing a particularly blistering set from Andy one weekend, we asked him how, when faced with so much vinyl to choose from, did he make choices in structuring his set. The answer we anticipated was something along the lines of just feeling it in the moment, but Andy revealed a method that was to be instrumental in the way that we structured theatre.

Over a three-hour set, Andy would begin with tracks with a tempo around 120 bpm (beats per minute). This was more than just a desire to start with a relatively pedestrian tempo – this was DJ etiquette. The DJ prior to Andy's set would, towards the end, slow the tempo down to something around 120 bpm in order to allow the incoming DJ to warm themselves up over a number of tracks as they became accustomed to the crowd. (120 bpm is the tempo for most pop and dance tracks and some theorists have gone to great lengths studying the effects this tempo has on the human body, pointing out that it is no coincidence that all the most popular pop and dance songs over the past 30 years sit within a range of 2 bpm difference.) Over the next 45 minutes, Andy would increase the bpm rate to around 140, drop it back to 120 over the next 15 minutes then build it up to a high of perhaps 145 over the next 30 minutes. This pattern would then repeat, forming a clear set of peaks and troughs before settling down and signing off when the DJing baton would be passed on to the incoming DJ at a sedate rate of 120 bpm. This was like a newfound science to us, instantly understandable as one that centred around the focus and capacity of a crowd/audience to be moved. For us, the mapping out of tempo like this was exactly the same as the rhythm we felt we needed to create for our own work – a rhythm that carried the audience along confidently, pushing them to points of intensity but also carrying them confidently out of that intensity, allowing breathing space and something like recovery or at least respite from events but all the while preparing the way for a further high or peak. On a good night, Andy's capacity to create an environment where he appeared totally in control was masterful and we wanted to achieve the same thing.

Taking the structure of a DJ set as laid out by Andy, we started to examine the existing scenes we had for *Klub*. One immediate realisation was that, unlike an incoming DJ, nobody was providing us with a handover. This had huge implications on our practice of creating a pre-show environment. We inverted Andy's model in order to fulfil what we needed at the start of our own work. Rather than building from a trough, *Klub* (and the following two shows *Flesh* and *Zero*) started with a peak, a physical sequence that was our equivalent of the 140 bpm track – full, hard, loud, exhilarating. From this point we allowed the rhythm of the show to settle for a while, allowing the audience to get the measure of the piece but with a steady sense of increasing pace leading up to a second physical sequence. It does not always follow that physical sequences and text scenes represented the peaks and troughs respectively. The intensity of a particular textual scene would be considered a peak and placed within the overall structure accordingly. Over the space of those first few shows (each one lasting approximately 75 minutes) there would be three peak scenes, one at the beginning, one somewhere near the middle and one as the penultimate scene. These would be the most intense points in the show and the rest of the piece would rise and fall between these points.

Another way in which music influenced the structure of our work was the running time of the scenes. For the Generation Trilogy, each scene lasted, on average, three and a half minutes, which is the running time of the average pop song. In this way, we aimed for the performances to be similar to watching MTV for an hour or so, a response to the prevailing theories in abundance at that time about the average attention span sitting within this time frame. This structural policy meant that each scene had to get to the point and conclude with precision and economy – no bad objective when devising material, be it textual, physical or a combination of the two.

As a creative device, we have used music to create soundtracks for every Frantic show. We use the term 'soundtrack' in an admitted nod towards its filmic implications. One reason for this is a term we use to describe the kind of music that we find particularly inspiring. That term is 'bedroom cinematic' and it is hard to describe exactly what this means but we know it when we hear it. It is often found in music that has a sense of the personal and yet involves the most lush, vast orchestration. A good starting point for discovering this type of music would be practically anything by the band Hybrid. It is in the throb of a punishing techno track that still has within it the sense of a heart breaking. Within these points there is an implicit sense of drama, which also might be a way of defining the essential element in music that we look for. Soundtracking also seems like an accurate term as many of the tracks we use are from existing film soundtracks. Film soundtracks are a very useful rehearsal tool. Many of them consist of short tracks and can often swing wildly from track to track in terms of mood. When improvising, we often use soundtracks like this as the aural wallpaper, an element for the performers to work along-side. The brevity of the tracks prevents the improvising performers getting lost in themselves and the irregular structural nature of the music means that people are not able to improvise in a way that they might do if using songs or music that follows the traditional verse/chorus/verse/chorus/middle eight/ chorus model. Performers are not always aware of using such structures, but this does not mean that they are not falling into the same rhythmic patterns on a subconscious level. Avoiding this makes for a purer improvisation that truly has to respond to the unexpected.

As with film scores, several Frantic shows have attempted to create a consistent sound and in this way create an arc, in the same way as one might consider the arc of a storyline. We have sometimes achieved this consistency by collaborating with a particular band or artist to provide all the music for a show. Working with the band lamb on *Peepshow* we were given access to their entire back catalogue plus stripped down versions of songs. These alternative versions are incredibly useful in being able to develop musical recurring themes throughout a show. We had eight versions of one particular track, 'Gabriel'. By associating the track with one of the couples in the show, we were able to map out their relationship in musical terms, using the full original version at the start of the show and then a pared down, strings-only version at the end as their relationship had unravelled. Even in the event of not having a single band or artist to source music from, we have still made precise choices on the type of music we intended to use. For *Sell Out* we used many tracks that featured piano and strings and also electronic tracks in a minor key in an attempt to locate those examples of electronica that somehow melt the heart. In the case of *Underworld*, we looked for tracks that were predominantly rich in percussion or strings. In creating the arc for the piece, we placed a track in the very middle of the show that acted as a kind of keystone. The track was the theme tune from the film *Unbreakable* by James Newton Howard and was used to backdrop a physical sequence in which all four female characters experience violent nightmares over one night. The track itself is a grand cinematic blast, full of menacing strings and snarling brass with possibly the creepiest break in soundtrack history, topped off with a thundering finale with quivering cellos and explosive percussion. Everything prior to this moment in the show in terms of music was building towards this apex, starting slowly with the pedestrian simplicity of Goldfrapp's 'Felt Mountain' track. Everything after this point was an exercise in progressive distortion, each track becoming more and more ominous and degraded now that the dam had burst both musically and dramatically. In this way, the score for the show genuinely has its own arc.

We have used the musical idea of the overture and translated it into a visual form. In music, the overture is the opening section that introduces themes used in the piece about to commence. The opening of *Underworld* was an erratic, violent stab of images, bursting out of the darkness and disappearing as soon as they were established. All the images were taken from scenes to come but were presented in no particular order in an attempt to appear disorientating and nightmarish. In this way, our visual overture sets the tone and prepares the audience for what is about to come without acting as a kind of spoiler for the events. In *Rabbit* we opened the second act with a short two-minute piece where we picked out the various characters involved in moments that we imagined had occurred during the time the audience had been out in the bar sipping gin and tonics while we hid in the toilets. The visual montage formed a visual bridge between the two acts, wordless and economical and not without a slightly sinister twist, given the events that were about to unfurl.

Selecting music is always a very personal, subjective and idiosyncratic process and in many ways is true of a particular creative view or feeling at a particular point in time. There are, however, a few constants in our choices. Many of our music choices have been instrumentals. One of the reasons for this is that instrumental tracks still allow for interpretation by the listener in a way that songs with sung lyrics do not. A lyric adds a specificity to a piece of music and in some instances this can have a reductive effect rather than enhancing a scene. On the occasions that we have used songs it is precisely because we are looking to create that specificity with the scene. We also try hard to avoid using music that most of our audience will already know or recognise. In listening to known music, we often start to bring to it our own associations. There is a danger here for an audience who might suddenly lose their place in the piece. The music and the scene in this instance have to work very hard to claim precedence in the mind of the audience member. Our choices have often involved orchestral pieces as well as hard industrial techno, both forms that are very 'big' in terms of sound. Given our proclivity for loud volume levels during performances, we are firm advocates of the 'big' sonic experience but we are also wary of not allowing music to overwhelm the scene. In the same way that the actor-to-set ratio is an important consideration for the way in which the entire show is received, so the music should never be at a level that outweighs the action or event it is supporting.

The idea of truly supporting the scene or event is one reason why we are cautious about using music that allows too much space to the point where it is difficult to see whether it is having any effect at all. Despite being ardent fans of ambient music, we are deeply suspicious of the all too common use of the soundscape in theatre. Again, this is a very subjective area, but the vagueness of certain music can leave a scene floundering. As with the combination of text and movement, the combination of scene and music should never result in the scene suddenly being made strange. Music choices are not always about harmony (there is much fun to be had creating musical counterpoints), but each music track has to justify itself. Despite occasional attempts, a track has never appeared in a Frantic show just because we were in love with it at the time. (Oh, all right, well maybe there was the post-show playout track for *Underworld*, but it was just an unforgivably brilliant remix . . .)

Listening to music can be a highly effective shorthand in the rehearsal room. Arguably, we would never have come up with such creepy, disturbing, dead body material for *Flesh* without the Nine Inch Nails track 'Closer (precursor)'. It is hard to imagine a more menacing piece of music and it is no surprise that the same track went on to be used by David Fincher to accompany the seminal title sequence for his film *Seven*. While creating a duet for the Bare Bones dance company, we asked the two performers to listen to Bjork's 'An Echo, A Stain' as a way of describing the movement quality we were looking for. The track has such a distinctive production quality that there is no danger of there being radically different interpretations of the mood evoked by such music. The vocal quality of the singer Sia, as featured on 'Destiny' by Zero 7, was used by us as a mood reference point during the making of *Peepshow*. Note it was the vocal quality that was important here although the lyrical content was also pertinent with references to 'watching porn in my hotel dressing gown'. To not flag up the vocal quality at play is to miss a trick in understanding the effectiveness of the line. In rehearsals for *pool (no water)* we played the cast 'Hide and Seek' by Imogen Heap and asked them to pay particular attention to the amount of silence and stillness throughout the track. While improvising the scene where the four friends go to visit their hospitalised friend for the very first time following a horrific accident, we asked them to reference the same quality of silence and stillness. The result was a scene of very precise choreography that was as much about not moving – a reference to and reflection of the song which often reduces itself to barely a breath.

The dynamic structures used in music arrangements are also a precious tool for us. During a workshop session for *Othello* the company listened to Hybrid's 'Just For Today' and in particular, a section towards the end of the track where a particular kick drum is heard on the 2 and 4 count of the odd numbered bars and then the 2, 4, 7 and 8 counts of the even bars. This structure is repeated four times. The sound quality of the drum is hard and brash and we asked the performers to create a string of material that not only used the impact points of the count structure but also the savage, tight sound of the drum sample as a reference point for the movement quality.

We have no restrictions when it comes to sourcing musical ideas. We are purists only in the sense that the end point is to serve dramatic purpose. The music itself is as likely to come from the *Finding Nemo* soundtrack as it is to come from a rare remixed version of an underground European techno house classic. One of the most beautiful and fragile tracks we found for *Underworld* came from Brad Fiedel's otherwise industrial score for *Terminator 2: Judgment Day*. An open mind and an open ear are essential when searching for existent music tracks to work with.

One of the most progressive art forms over the last twenty years has been the music video. The marriage of music with images has become one of the most inspiring and invigorating practices, mini cinematic events that cram the epic into a four-minute gem. The visual techniques employed have been seminal in developing the ways that we read visual information and the editing techniques of directors such as Chris Cunningham are spectacular. In trying to understand effective use of music choices for theatre, it is probably best to look to music video directors such as Chris Cunningham, Michel Gondry, Jonathan Glaser, Mark Romanek and Spike Jonze. Of course, these artists are given the music track first and then look to create the scene around it but, in looking at the results they create, one can see the incredible outcome when music and images coalesce effectively.

Music sits at the very heart of our creative process. On many, many occasions, an idea has sprung from the conversation that starts with 'I was listening to this track and, I don't know why, but this image came into my head and . . . ' Our relationship with music is an ongoing artistic development though there is a recognised Frantic-style track. We only know this as we have regularly had people tell us that they have heard a track and have thought it to be 'very Frantic'. It's pleasing to discover that, in most cases, they are absolutely right.

Frantic and film

At the time of writing we are by no means the only company who display obvious signs of filmic influence in presenting work on stage. At this point it is important that we make a distinction between two different types of work. Certain work will actively include film as part of the theatrical image. Artists such as Wim Wandekeybus, Robert Lepage and Théâtre De Complicité have all demonstrated the incredible results that can occur when the two forms are effectively drawn together. As a company we have been less interested in using film on stage and more obsessed with using the stylistic devices and techniques of film making and trying to create work on stage that embraces these practices. These include principles of editing, how images are framed, how to control the focus of the viewer, the use of music to soundtrack a story, how scenes are ordered and their interrelation, the specificity of filmic narrative and the implications of a specific colour palette. As always, our search for such inspiration takes us from the loftiest heights of arthouse classics to multiplex no-brainers. We are likely to spend hours discussing the semiotic brilliance of *Star Wars* (dir. George Lucas, 1977) in much the same way as discussing the extraordinary colour schemes of Wong Kar Wei's *In the Mood for Love* (2000). We felt no shame when asking Dick Bird to consider the architecture featured in *Lethal Weapon 2* (dir. Richard Donner, 1989) during pre-production meetings for *Rabbit*. Similarly we are just as happy introducing any creative member of the Frantic team to the phenomenal editing techniques of director Chris Cunningham. Following the immediate inspiration from Volcano Theatre

Company it was film rather than theatre that encouraged us to form a company in an attempt to create work like that which we were seeing. Watching David Hinton's seminal dance films for DV8, *Dead Dreams of Monochrome Men* (1990) and *Strange Fish* (1992), is probably one of the most important moments in our cultural lives and we are convinced we are not the only artists who owe their dues to these immaculate works of art.

To begin with, we did implement film into the theatrical mix, albeit in a very lo-fi manner. Our second Edinburgh foray with William M. Hoffman's *As Is* in 1992 involved projected images of highly controversial S&M activity during the opening physical sequence. Our touring production of *Look Back in Anger* in 1994 featured two old-style TV sets at both sides of the stage that flashed up various sentences from Douglas Coupland's novel *Generation X* (Abacus, 1991). Both of these were fairly unsatisfactory. After this, the move into the Generation Trilogy took the focus away from such literal uses of found images and we found ourselves far more invigorated by the form and technique of film than the actual use of it on stage. As the budgets for these shows were shock-ingly small, our choice to drop the pursuit of film on stage was not wholly one of creative disinterest. It was a toss up between hiring a video projector for an entire tour or a cast of four being able to afford trainers that were made of something slightly more comfortable and practical than reconstituted tyre treads. In hindsight, the choice was a good one though the trainers were still cheap and did nothing for our knees and ankles.

The two shows where film was used were *Tiny Dynamite* and *On Blindness* – both shows being co-productions. We were collaborating with Vicky Featherstone (at that time Artistic Director for Paines Plough) and designer Julian Crouch on *Tiny Dynamite*, and Julian was eager to work with projections that moved rather than moving film. In this way, the effect would stay within the lo-fi style as favoured by Julian but would also take the image beyond the static. The effect within the show was truly beautiful. Julian had a very sensitive eye for the details of the moving projections in the piece that was a major part of the overall delicacy of the show. He also, wherever possible, projected onto vital elements within the scenes. A flurry of images of car tail-lights were projected onto a large white sheet of paper to suggest the road trip the two friends embark upon at the beginning of the show. Gently pulsing images of electrical storms were presented on one character's body as he began to describe the anger felt towards his dearest friend, echoing the central theme of lightning strikes. A handkerchief held in the air caught, for a brief moment, a full moon as a summer night's party reached its peak. In all cases, the pro-jected images were subsumed as deeply as possible into the set. In this way, they were 'crowd pleasers' that in no way overshadowed the onstage event. Instead, they were embedded in the *mise-en-scène*, minute moments of magic that drew little if any comment from the onstage characters.

Steven Hoggett on stage in *On Blindness*, 2004

For *On Blindness* we reunited with Vicky and Julian and were also joined by Jenny Sealey of Graeae Theatre Company. The show centred around ideas of perception. One strand of the story featured an artist revealing a painting of a nude to the sitter for the first time. The other centred around a first date scenario shared by a blind woman and a man whose job was to audio describe films for blind audiences. Julian's set idea consisted of two large canvases, one suspended at the back and a similar-sized canvas that was the floor of the playing space. Again, the visual element was something closer to moving projections and transcribed text rather than film. It was felt that the dynamic of film would detract from the energy, aesthetic and feel of the scenes being performed. Each projected sequence had to earn its place within the show and be seen to enhance rather than upstage or provide an interesting distraction during a scene change.

These two shows aside, the uses of film for us have been many and varied but not in the literal sense. On occasion we have used film to dictate the entire effect of a show upon its audience. Discussing the possible impact of *pool (no water)* with Mark Ravenhill, we were trying to decide how best to present a cast of characters who, it might be argued, demonstrated levels of heinous and unforgivable behaviour from start to finish. For inspiration we referred to the classic scene from Alfred Hitchcock's *Psycho* that totally implicates the audience into being onside with a character during an act of pure atrocity. Following the seminal scene where Janet Leigh comes to grief in the shower, we follow the events as Norman Bates dumps her body in the boot of his car. Driving out to a swamp, he steps out of the car before pushing it into the swamp. At first, it seems that all is going to plan, the car quickly sinking into the mud with satisfying gurgling sounds. However, the car is only half submerged when it suddenly stops. The camera cuts back to Norman, already anxiously looking around for fear of being witnessed and biting his nails (not the subtlest moment of physicality in cinema, agreed, but it was 1960 after all). The camera cuts back to the car which is still going nowhere, at which point the audience, without realising the implications, are all willing that car to sink. Knowing the body is in the boot and knowing the full submergence of the car completes the effectiveness of the crime, Hitchcock pulls a fantastic trick by making us complicit with the criminal. After another cut to our Norman (for at this point he really is ours, we share his anxiety and will for the event to complete), the camera returns to the car that, after another second or two, resumes its descent to the swamp floor with a return of satisfying gurgling. Norman's relief is ours and Hitchcock becomes a genius. Whether *pool (no water)* achieved and maintained this onside sentiment with its protagonists is open to opinion. It is enough to point out that this cinematic moment became a constant reference point for us in how we chose to develop the play and then direct it for the stage.

Creating choreographic unison out of seemingly random bodies is a frequent event on the Frantic stage and almost every example of this takes its influence from the film *Boogie Nights* (dir. Paul Thomas Anderson, 1997). There is a majestic scene halfway through the film where the newly named protagonist, Dirk Diggler, takes to the dancefloor and, resplendent in his newly acquired seventies garb, kicks off some classic disco moves. Within moments, the rest of the dancefloor fall in with Dirk and there ensues a glorious unison sequence that even manages to include a roller-skating waitress. The sequence itself is probably only 20 seconds long but the way in which the scene opens out is a true Frantic favourite. It is a moment of pure unison where a collective of individuals discover themselves united in a moment. In this instance, it is the pinnacle of the porn industry in the late seventies before the advent of video and the dark days of cocaine addiction. The shared physicality marks the unity and happiness of the group and serves as a sharp contrast to the disparate lives that are about to ensue as a decade of greed shatters the relationships among a group of porn industry friends.

Some of the most exhilarating and progressive examples of modern film making take the form of music videos. Michel Gondry's epic for Massive

Attack's 'Protection' (1995) was a huge inspiration for our production *Peepshow*. As a creative team, we all looked to it as a source for ideas. This ranged from the metallic finish Dick Bird designed in our elevator to the colour palette that inspired Natasha Chivers in lighting the four bedrooms. The journey of the camera in and around the bedrooms of the tower block was heavily informative in the way that we as directors selected scenes and their duration. Even minute details like the passing of a passenger jet in the background was something that we referenced in our show as a rare reminder of the expansive world outside. In the music video, the camera rarely passes through a door. Instead it stealthily glides in through a number of windows. This voyeuristic quality was also one that we employed when rehearsing the show with lighting states softly lifting on scenes that always gave the impression of not quite starting at the beginning. In this way we turned the audience into voyeurs, the unsettling feeling of having chanced on a scene already in progress enhancing the sense that there had been no invitation to witness the events that were happening. The occasional surreal events that Gondry discovers in some of the rooms gave us the courage to create our own scenes of heightened realism. One such scene involved a couple love making in a bed where, in accordance with the jealous and suspicious mindset of the man, a third body, a male neighbour, kept mysteriously appearing in the middle of their physical duet among the sheets only to keep disappearing back into the bed. A verbal argument between one couple saw them explode out of their room and tumble up, around and through all the other bedrooms, taking their argument with them as they fought through walls and ceilings (reminiscent of Jonathan Glazer's 2002 'Odyssey' TV advert for Levi Jeans).

Our creative bravery has often come from film makers' own acts of audacious brilliance. Paul Thomas Anderson does nothing to prepare his audience for the moment in *Magnolia* (1999) where the entire ensemble cast share the singing duties of Aimee Mann's 'Wise Up'. Up until this point we have been following the lives of nine separate characters over one day in the San Fernando Valley. So far, so epic. Music is used throughout in the conventional way until one song which is being listened to by an estranged daughter. Alone in her room, she snorts a line of cocaine during the first line of the song and by the second line, we hear her sing along. Midway through the same verse the film cuts to another character this time not visibly listening to the song via radio or any discernible source. However, he picks up the song at the point where we left the estranged daughter. This method plays out through the entire song through all nine characters. As a narrative device it is perfect, the point at which the sentiment of the lyrics is shared by each of the characters. The event itself makes complete sense in terms of content but the form it takes is both radical and exhilarating. That the device is neither referred to nor repeated only adds to the virtuosity of the decision. We knew that we wanted the cast to sing full-length songs during *Peepshow* and the prospect of this was incredibly daunting to us. Watching this scene for the first time unlocked both our understanding and eagerness towards the idea. Anderson brazenly introduces a whole new language to his audience and it is immediately accepted and embraced. This was our challenge in presenting our own musical *Peepshow*. To this day, we cite this scene in the same way that people refer to Yves Klein's famous fall from a wall onto the pavement below – a clear and brilliant moment of artistic bravery. During a very recent discussion planning a large and ambitious devised show that we were involved with, the director talked of wanting to create their '*Magnolia* moment'. Without knowing exactly what this might be or how we might make it, the one certainty is that we all know what it means.

During a film course at The Place in London in 2004, David Hinton provided a dazzling insight into the ways in which film and movement coexist. As well as a detailed examination of his films for DV8 he also provided a whirlwind tour throughout the history of dance on film. This ranged from *Singin' in the Rain* (dir. Stanley Donen, Gene Kelly, 1952) and *West Side Story* (dir. Jerome Robbins, Robert Wise, 1961) through to dance films from Rosemary Butcher and David's own controversial, award-winning *Birds* (2000). It was interesting, particularly when looking at more modern examples, how the films were falling into two distinct categories. One was where the dance performance was exactly as it appeared on the stage and the other was where the camera seemed to have been considered in either the making or, in some cases, the remaking of the choreography. When watching dance on film now, it is interesting how it is rarely the former that interests us. It is only when movement truly engages with the form of film that we are held, intrigued and inspired. This does not detract from the thrill we might get from, say, the filmed version of Pina Bausch's *Rite of Spring*, but this is more to do with the formidable power of this work as a piece of dance theatre. Arguably, there is little that film could do to better the effectiveness of this classic.

Some of the golden rules of film making suggested by David have been embraced by Frantic to become part of our structuring principles when devising theatre. One example was how, when cutting from one shot to another, there should be a difference of approximately 30 percent in terms of the framing of the shot. An example of this would be to go from a close-up to a mid-shot. This sense of variety and comparison in composition is one that we use in mapping out the visual arc of our work. A sequence in *Stockholm* where the couple career gleefully around the kitchen was followed by a tight spotlit moment on top of the kitchen counter. The expansive sequence Caterpillar from *Hymns* that saw the entire stage washed in huge, celestial light was followed by a scene we called Guyscrapers with two performers perched on a ladder as high as the venue would allow in pale, precise lighting. The use of lighting is

A close-up of Georgina Lamb, *Stockholm*, 2007

essential in creating such a dynamic on stage and should be considered and utilised at all times.

Film provides a phenomenally efficient shorthand in the rehearsal room. For *Dirty Wonderland* we had just four weeks to create our most ambitious show that travelled through a hotel comprising literally hundreds of bedrooms. It also took place in a ballroom, a dining room, a bar, a kitchen, a reception area and various corridors. One scene took place in a room that was totally blacked out so that the walls and therefore the limits of the room were invisible. We wanted this room to be like the epicentre of the most hardcore club and for the cast to be in the throes of something ecstatic. We were trying to describe the sense of physical energy we thought this space and scene would need and were struggling to find the right words. It would have been against our choreographic principles to demonstrate in front of the company. To us, this is akin to giving an actor a reading of the line as you would like them to do it – a rehearsal room crime. Instead, we showed the company two Missy Elliott videos. Her work with director Hype Williams has produced some truly innovative choreography, which is as much about the editing technique he employs as the actual moves themselves. We asked the cast to look at the way in which the physical energy of the choreography constantly seemed to give the impression of pulling inwards. Limbs in these videos did not fling outwards so much as roll and bounce towards an eternally accepting centre. It was, and still is, a quality at odds with the usual pop video choreographic style where shapes are sharp and all about exertion. Here, the physicality seemed to be something closer to constant regeneration. We spent only moments describing our thoughts on this after the viewing. The full company immediately understood the ballpark we were working in and in one afternoon we created and constructed the entire sequence for the show. In this instance, we were lucky enough to have a cast who were capable of taking a starting point and allowing it to truly challenge their own style of moving and produce results that were both brand new and yet true to the originating idea.

In comparison to theatre, film will always be a greater influence on our work, not least of all because we see more of it than theatre shows. It also fascinates us because it poses constant challenges in trying to emulate its brilliant moments of effectiveness. Referencing other works of theatre is simply theft. Referencing film we like to think of as slightly less criminal, not least of all because, in our experience, it takes a lot more thought, time and effort. The nature of theatre often means that such ideas have to undergo various transformations in the process. In this way, the process is often a healthy challenge to one's creative ability.

chapter two

Scenes and their creation

This chapter highlights scenes from Frantic Assembly shows, describing the devising process behind each of them. These scenes have been performed hundreds of times and have taught us much about the processes behind them and how we might have developed them. More importantly this chapter suggests how you might develop them.

To facilitate this, each scene will be looked at from three perspectives:

- The Idea – the inspiration behind the scene and what we wanted to achieve
- The Process – how we created the scene
- The Development – how **you** might develop the process. Any process is not forever linked to the end product. It can be adjusted and reused. This section explores the future potential of the process.

Each scene is named as it was in the production. That in itself is a clue to our devising history. Each scene was named because the structure of the production was up for grabs. Initially we were not making work from a script. Each scene needed a name so that we could refer to it quickly when trying to work out the order of the production.

The names are personal. Some of them are obvious (Exhaustion), some of them are obscure (Guyscrapers). All the names were merely functional descriptions of the scenes we had created. They were our code or shorthand.

Refer to the Anthology section in the Introduction for more details on each production.

Lullaby

This scene is called Lullaby after the music track used ('Lullaby' by lamb from the album *Fear of Fours*). See 'Accidents and creativity' (page 26) for more details of how the track came to be used.

The Idea

The set for *Hymns* consisted of five chairs and one strong metal table, surrounded by a construction of ladders. Four men sit around the table. Previously they have laughed and joked their way out of the funeral, through several bottles of beer, and now find themselves with very little to say. This is a moment of introspection after the macho bravado of their reunion.

Lullaby is about time passing and not a word being said. A friend has died and all that has been shared are jokes and beers. We wanted a scene that captures the extended introspection of the hours following the funeral where the information of the day slowly starts to sink in.

A moment of introspection in *Hymns*, 2005

The Process

Lullaby is a series of opportunities for connections between the four guys sitting in chairs around a large table. At times their actions attract each other. At others they repel. As one person moves forward to possibly speak, address, or even touch their mate that person is pushed or feels compelled to move away. Why? What do they fear from those connections? What would the touch mean? What can of worms would it open?

The first thing we played with was stillness and potential. This had to be a scene where the tiniest movement could be explosive, so we had to start from stillness rather than action. From the stillness the performers were asked to find fairly naturalistic but precise moves that involved resting their arms on the table, resting their heads, touching their face, looking at their hands. They were insular and fairly abstracted moves.

When one performer moves it has a physical consequence on the other. It might push or it might pull them. They do not touch but what makes them connect is the feeling of the move. More specifically it comes from starting and stopping at the same time even though the moves are different. For example, one character might brush dust off his trousers and fold his arms while another might be compelled to look at his hands and then place them on the table. If both characters' actions start and finish together, it emphasises not only the actions but also the return to stillness. The stillness is once again filled with potential. The sense that the men want to connect but are terrified to do so, or be seen to be trying to, returns.

This is the choreographed scene in its simplest form. We then started to play with the focus of the audience. Instead of all characters stopping together we tried one character continuing on their own and found that they now commanded all the attention. We played with connections across space. We had one person sit back in their chair as their connection with another character opposite appeared to pull that person forward in their chair. We played with levels of action. We went from the focus of a single hand moving across a table to the frenetic readjustments of all the characters in their chairs and then returned to a perfectly timed stillness. All of this was then shaped by the particular and peculiar rhythms of our choice of music. This dictated when we used the material that we had found. It was the structure that the physicality was placed on. We also found moments of focus on each of the characters and the lighting picked them out accordingly. This allowed the scene to present a group unified in grief but also individuals lost and alone as they contemplate their friend's death and the newly forming dynamic of the remaining friendships.

The Development

The basic task within this process is to find connections between people's movements. We opted to keep it mostly small and slow. This fitted our theme. The process itself could support other themes and contexts.

The process highlights tension between people. Tension can be a positive or a negative. Within *Hymns* it was about people with emotions to hide, desperate to avoid being asked to talk about them. The process could just as easily portray sexual tension. It is all about changing the context.

Try following the process above and choreographing a scene between, say, two potential lovers. Run the material created to make sure they are secure in their knowledge of moves.

Decide on a piece of music to accompany it. Get to know the music and begin to tie down the moves to the music (you are not necessarily changing the moves. Maybe just noting when they happen within the music).

Now create two rooms and place the two characters in a room each. Instruct them to sit oblivious to the presence of the other in the next room. Run the scene and see whether their physicality can still connect while they are separated by the 'wall' between them.

What if the characters were aware of each other, longed for each other but could not be together? Run the material again to see whether the moves have a greater or different resonance.

Headwrecker   *Hymns 1999/2005*

The Idea

Headwrecker was a physical sequence that followed the line 'We could just talk' as the four friends who have come together to mourn the passing of their mutual friend struggle to genuinely connect. The idea was that each of them, on hearing the request, slips into the kind of conversation that men might find easy. Such language would be incredibly informed and detailed but reveal little or nothing about the speaker. To 'just talk' is easy. To talk about what matters and be prepared to listen to the uncomfortable truths contained is another matter.

Steven Hoggett, Joseph Traynor, Karl Sullivan and Eddie Kay having their heads wrecked, *Hymns*, 2005

The Process

To start with, the four performers were each given one of four conversational topics – car maintenance, stereo technical specifications, traffic directions and commentary on a football match. Choreographer and director Liam Steel then developed text for each of these topics before the four of us were introduced to the track 'Petite Fleur' by Chris Barber's Jazz Band. We were asked to sit the entire text within four bars of music. For some of us, this meant talking at an incredibly rapid pace while for others, the tempo was far more laid back and casual. The point here was to refrain from using the strict rhythm of the music track to inform the rhythm of the spoken words. Instead, we were to make the words sound as casual and natural as possible. This very simple step took a considerable amount of time. Counting the bars in order to fit within the four-bar limit instinctively led us to create weird rhythms and inflections that took some ironing out.

We were then asked to create a gestural string of movement to accompany our words. The moves were to be quite heavily influenced by the music and its count structure. In being a gestural string, the emphasis was on the hands, arms and torso with the feet remaining fixed. We were also asked to remain facing front for the duration of our sequence. Finally combining the two, words and gestural string, was possibly one of the most frustrating periods of any Frantic rehearsal. We were at the end of the rehearsal period and all very tired and bruised. Our brains were full of counts, lines and motivations and this sudden, seemingly simple task proved too much for each one of us at some time or another. As frustrating as it was, this period was also a formidable bonding experience as the remaining three would pick up the wailing boy from the floor where we all at one time collapsed. The result, however, was absolutely right. A fluid combination of words and text that taught us much about the steps required in combining the two. The tight, detailed choreography sat completely at ease alongside a very casual, believable delivery of words. Knowing that this was within our grasp we spent every spare second (there were about eight of them we think) practising together – in the bathroom, in the canteen, walking to work.

Just when we thought we had it nailed, Liam then introduced a collective task. This was an eight-bar text that looked at the comparisons between the body of a woman and the body of a car along with a whole new gestural sequence. Upon realising this was the request, it's possible that most if not all of us wanted to take hold of a large hammer and cause some serious damage. However, an interesting lesson is the human capacity to push the limits of their self-imposed restrictions. In suddenly having a whole new section to worry about, the previous section no longer seemed like the problem. Simply thinking this turned it into a reality – it really wasn't the problem and it instantly stopped being one. Our capacity to get that third count right in the sixth bar was extraordinary. As for the new section, the first few attempts brought fresh tears but we were on a roll now and in one afternoon we had something that, while not being presentable, was at least respectable.

Liam pulled the same trick the following day (and to repeat some of the comments made between the four of us would do some serious damage to what continues to be a very loving and respectful relationship) but the effect was exactly the same. The Car/Woman section was forced to fall into place as the new section – a combined and fractured combination of all four narratives – took precedence. The following day (the day before the show actually opened), when Liam added in a new unison section, we were so attuned to the demands of the task that we had it down in 20 minutes.

Having completed the sequence, we thought it fitting to give it the name Headwrecker. Even well into the tour, Headwrecker would feature the most spectacular mistakes. In presenting the scene, the four of us would climb onto a small table with two at the front and two close behind. The interweaving individual sections were underpinned by moments of extremely tight unison, not least of all spatially. Any errors up there were glaring and Headwrecker always required maximum concentration to get through the four minutes without suddenly getting eye contact with someone who you had never spotted before doing that move. One tiny error and suddenly somebody's spark plug move was swinging into your humpbacked bridge moment. Climbing down off the table after a clean run of Headwrecker never failed to be a moment of pure collective joy.

The Development

An obvious development of this exercise is to suddenly introduce language that does have emotional weight and resonance. What might this do to the movement? Does the leaking of personal, internal thoughts lead to empowerment or does the realisation that the truth is flooding out lead to something like a breakdown? Does the body resist in an effort to shut down this unravelling?

There are many themes and ideas that might be used in place of the textual ideas we used for Headwrecker. Looking at the characters specific to the piece being created will dictate the kind of text that might be used for this exercise. Our decision to sound like our dads is a very simple one at heart. The perceived notion of how difficult men find it to communicate is not so simple an issue, but in looking at a simple starting point we work our way closer to the central idea of the scene.

As ever, play with pace and rhythm. Try different music once you have the material down. Consider the flippant, blokey atmosphere Headwrecker created. What would the effect be if you had one of the characters, separate from the others, going through his lines and moving quietly on his own? Does the group scene become undermined? Is it a moment of unity or is it a tiresome practised ritual?

A perfect example of devising to the end?

Headwrecker came late into the rehearsal process for a reason. Director Liam Steel did not keep it tucked up his sleeve just to cause pain in the production week. We were already at a point of running what we thought was the complete show when we all recognised that it was getting stuck in a mire somewhere in the middle. The pace became turgid. The mood became excessively heavy. It felt indulgent. This was a crime, not only against theatricality, but against the subject matter. We were determined that if we were going to make a show about men grieving and not feeling like they have the platform to air their real thoughts, then it must never seem indulgent. This would see the whole theme dismissed by the audience and would make the show pointless.

Headwrecker came about through the need for light relief. We needed something to break the tension, to make the audience laugh and feel refreshed. We also needed the characters to believe that their flippancy had got them off the hook ('we could just talk') for a moment before their world comes crashing down again later. Otherwise the show was all one rhythm.

This is an example where we got the judgement right. This is not always the case (see 'Stockholm Fight', page 84).

Slabslammers *Hymns 1999/2005*

The set for this scene consisted of five chairs and one strong metal table surrounded by a construction of ladders reaching up as far as the ceiling would allow.

The Idea

We talked about the finality of death, how it turns the people we know into bodies of meat and utterly devoid of life. This scene is about the four guys struggling to come to terms with this finality. They are also disturbed and fascinated by the new group dynamic. There are four of them occupying five chairs. We wanted their dead friend to be present through his absence.

The Process

There was no easy way into this scene. Now that the performers were at the peak of fitness and confidence almost anything could be asked of them. This scene required no trickery, just bravery and technique. The performers ran and flew into the air, landing as flat and 'meat' like as they could. Director Liam

Steel was looking for that immediate contrast between the life and vitality of the jump and the inanimate quality of the landing. This is where the thought lies. This is where the characters would be saying, in a split second, all the words we felt it was awkward to say verbally.

As the characters share these thoughts yet do not articulate them with each other, Liam wanted to create a scene where the action of one character, i.e. him crashing his body onto the hard metal table, was quickly replaced by another character doing the very same. The performers improvised their own journey around the table, looking for moments to cross over with another character and replace him on the table. We were looking for the most exciting and apparently reckless crossovers as the characters pushed themselves harder and harder towards an understanding of the physical quality of being meat on a slab.

Once this choreography was completed the scene was then set to a piece of music that initially felt impossibly short, our task being to fit all the moves into the length of the music. This meant that the moves always had that initial drive behind them. Our instinct when we are making work is to do something we are only just capable of. This always gave us something to aim for and we never really got up to speed until the opening night. Even then the slightest mistake would mean that it would be impossible to keep within the music. This effectively raised the stakes for this scene, gave it an edge and kept it fresh.

The Development

It would be foolish to think you could recreate this scene straight off without the training and a suitably strong and safe set. There is, however, an alternative to crashing down on the table with such force. Maybe it is a moment where the energy drops and a character curls onto the table as a bed, only to burst back to life and be replaced by another character having a similar moment. The most important consideration is this: What does that moment of stillness signify? What is going on in the private world of the character on the table? This is the heart of the piece. Without that it is only ever going to be a physical spectacle.

Consider, also, the focus on the fifth chair. Who is missing? What happens if you place a person in that chair constantly throughout the movement, keeping still as everyone else crashes around them? Who are they? Are their thoughts any different from those of the characters landing on the table? What happens if you take that chair away completely? What have you lost or gained?

What if you were to alter the setting? The set offered us so much in terms of physical support and in that our actions were contrasting with the naturalistic actions associated with the table and chairs. The table gets reinvented as a mortuary slab through the actions of the performers. It conjures up images of Da Vinci's *The Last Supper*, of death and betrayal. Would another setting offer this kind of transition and wealth of associations?

This is, of course, slightly academic as you should be looking to see if this process is applicable to the setting that you already have. It is this primary setting that is most important as this helps define the social rules, context and subtext. For example, if four men are sitting around a table and are not talking, we might sense there is a problem. If the four men are sitting in an Underground tube carriage and not talking, we might not assume there is a problem.

Sunbathers   *Tiny Dynamite 2001*

The Idea

This scene was created during the rehearsals for *Tiny Dynamite*. It suggests bodies at luxurious rest during an idyllic summer. The three characters involved have spent long, sunny hours together and have reached a point of comfort and ease with one another – the thrill and joy that they share is based on the sense that there is no urgency in their lives. With daily routines that involve simply food, swimming and sunbathing, the three have fallen into a collective pattern of behaviour. Sunbathers was an attempt to present the passing of such hours and their cumulative effect on Madeleine, Anthony and Lucien.

The Process

The set for the show was a square of decking (much like the outdoor decking that had featured so heavily in Channel 4's *Big Brother* that summer). Using the square as our performing space, the three of us started by creating a short, simple string of material based around the idea of positions assumed during sunbathing.

This initial material was kept low key. All the material took place on the floor and focused on shifts of position concentrating on elbows, stretches and adjusting the body to absorb the warmth of the sunshine. We avoided extraneous elements such as suntan lotion, wiping perspiration from the brow, archetypal mime. Instead, we looked at the kinds of behaviour rarely afforded without spending long hours with nothing more to do other than enjoy stillness and heat. This included things like suddenly finding a fascination in the cracked skin just visible between two toes and the sensation of sweat in the crook of an arm. Once we had established this string of material we added all three together, creating linking moments between the sections where necessary. This string was then learnt by all of us to discover the natural rhythms and pulses within the sequence.

For some time now, we had used a video camera to record improvisations and scenes in the rehearsal room and one of the qualities we always liked was that seen when rewinding a recording at a slow speed. Movement viewed in this way has a fantastic capacity for 'arrest' – a very hard and clean stopping motion that finishes the action when seen in reverse.

Using this idea, we then learnt the sunbathing scene in reverse, taking care to observe what happens to the rhythm in reverse and, in particular, looking out for the arrest points, these almost unnatural stopping points. The sequence was played out in unison and a later development was inserting moments where the three would look across at one another as though in acknowledgement of the synchronicity of their lives, the ease with which they connected with one another and the shared impulses that come from time spent together.

To punctuate the idea that this was a sequence in reverse, we finally added a moment at the very end where, still in unison, all three characters removed a strawberry from their mouths, an action that marked the beginning of the sequence in real time. This moment became something of a 'crowd pleaser' but was notable for us as being an exercise in tongue control. Executing the sequence with a large strawberry in your mouth, which you are desperately trying to hide from the audience, was something of a challenge. Trying not to choke on it was one thing. Making sure you didn't remove a red pulp from your mouth, indistinguishable as a strawberry, was something altogether different.

The Development

For *Tiny Dynamite* we wanted to show a trio at a point of subliminal unity, an emotional harmony that, with the glances between them, is acknowledged and relished. For us, unison from start to finish was seen as the best way to portray this as we wanted to pinpoint the action well into the summer. However, an immediate development of this exercise would be to play with breaking into or out of unison. Each performer might start by being involved in their own string and then actually play out the moments during which they realise that they are sharing a place, a time, a sentiment, a response and this realisation might start to align them in their movements.

Spatially, it might be of interest to create the material as explained here but, once the material has been created, try to run the same string, this time sitting in a chair or even a hammock and seeing what opportunities and complexities come from trying to remain as faithful to the original string as possible.

As a movement sequence, it is of the type that would be easily set with dialogue, although it is important to note that, for us, it was the unspoken complicity between the three that was important to convey.

In performance, there was a genuine sense of play between the three and so another development might be for the sequence to almost become a challenge, with the actual movements becoming more and more complex. In this way, the characters are seen to enjoy the sport inherent within their discovery. The sequence then turns into an exploration of how far they can go in sync with one another before one of them breaks.

Heavenly Legs   *Heavenly 2002*

The Idea

The audience have their perspective changed and look down on three men sitting in a waiting room in Heaven. The audience feel they are watching the men from above. The men are on a sofa and their mindless twitching and bored adjustments becomes a choreographed dance for legs. It was a lighthearted observation of the patterns of behaviour the three men adopted as they passed the time and tried not to get on each other's nerves.

The Process

The process should have been simple but it caught us at a bad time. We were exhausted and our brains were in meltdown. We sat in three chairs placed in a row. We improvised some playful choreography with our legs crossing and uncrossing, draping them over and flicking them off each other, kicking them out and twitching them. We filmed these doodles until we could cherry-pick moments that were funny or clever.

We already had a piece of music in mind so we started placing our rough material within the track. We decided to match the dynamic of the music quite closely at times and more so towards the end. The choreography should initially appear accidental and haphazard but then become more and more Esther Williams. We hoped this would achieve a comic effect.

There was a crucial third part to the process. The intention of the scene was to present a new perspective for the audience to observe the characters from. To do that the action must take place on the inverted sofa placed 10 feet up the back wall of the set (as shown in the image of *Heavenly*, in the colour plate section). This was a mirror illusion of the sofa on the floor. To achieve the illusion of gravity we had to perform it on our backs with our legs in the air. We had to keep our necks very straight and maintain little naturalistic looks and gestures. We started by inverting chairs until we had the 'luxury' of trying it on the set.

This was one of the most painful and gruelling physical scenes in any Frantic Assembly show. During the tour our stomach muscles became defined and our necks bulked up with muscle. Not once did anyone ever show appreciation for the physical strength and stamina involved. That was because the illusion was so successful. It really did look like we were just sitting in a sofa larking around while the audience watched from above us!

The Development

The initial idea and process shows quite a bit of creative development. To explore the further theatrical development we suggest that you take it back to chairs sat on the floor and play with the context within which the choreography is presented.

Give your group some time to create their material. Remember that people will normally give you more than you will need so stress with the participants that they should only use their legs (think *Riverdance*) and not set out to tell a story. Keep it fairly simple and have around 18 moves between the group of 3. Avoid predictable patterns and rhythms and make sure they are not working to counts.

Now show the material. Is it fast enough? Do they know it well enough? Is it clear enough? It needs to be slick and well practised. Ideally they should be able to loop the material until you want them to stop.

At this stage it is only choreography.

Now give one group three newspapers to read so that we do not see their faces. Choose a music track and run the scene. Does a story emerge?

Tell another group to rest against each other as if asleep. Play a different track. Let their legs spring into life as they sleep on the chairs (park bench?).

Get another group and ask for a volunteer to walk around the room staring at them. The three have to stare back at the walker as their legs carry on the routine. Change the music. How has this changed the story? Is it provocative? Flirtatious?

Now for a more complex development. Get a group to sit in the chairs, preferably a group we have already seen. It is always useful to see our opinions of the meaning of choreography change in front of our eyes!

Ask them to go through their routine as slowly as they can. Make two of them stare at one of the performers sat on the outside of the three. They should look right at them throughout but the third performer must keep looking straight ahead. That is, until a single moment when they can fleetingly return the look to their colleagues. The colleagues must maintain the look throughout. Try a new track. Or try one you have already tried. Does it or the choreography become redefined by the new direction? What is the story? Is it more complex? Is it a love triangle? Is it bullying? Is it funny? Is it scary?

Try presenting the choreography in a more literal context. The initial intention to show subconscious patterns of behaviour in moments of tedium can relate directly to many literal contexts – a dentist's waiting room, a tube train, etc.

The animated audience

There is another way to create work through a similar process. This time let the groups of three create a string of material that does not involve physical interaction. It can also involve the top half. It is about creating unison and you can use the literal physicality of the waiting room as a starting point. They can cross legs, uncross, adjust, lean forward, back, fold their arms, pick fluff from their clothes, clean their glasses, stretch, etc. The task is to turn it into a creative string of choreography.

If you have bleacher seating or any kind of raked seating, you can now place the whole group randomly around the auditorium. They are all now watching a show. Their focus must express this but they continue to perform their string, still aiming for unison with partners they are no longer next to.

Place yourself on the stage opposite them. Film them if possible. Play with the dynamic. Is it best slow? Or a freestyle mixture? It it just a mess or is the camera picking up some happy accidents? Have the relationships been blown apart or do they still exist over space? Are there new relationships and fleeting connections being formed? You can share these discoveries with the group and quickly try out new dynamics.

This exercise creates a large group scene without having to manage the whole group. They have been broken up into bite-sized groups and given simple tasks. You then bring them back together and shape the overall choreography.

Select Delete   *pool (no water) 2006*

The Idea

Select Delete marked the final act of atrocity committed by four would-be artists upon their hapless one-time friend. In terms of text, it consisted of the words 'select delete' repeated 47 times as the characters deleted one image after another from a computer file and, in doing so, ruined the creative efforts of their ailing fifth member. After a variety of read-throughs, a turning point was established by introducing the Imogen Heap track 'Mic Check' to sit alongside the scene. Previous attempts to unravel the repetition seemed to fail – probably due to the heavy, malicious intentions we were playing with. 'Mic Check', with its slick, playful, jittering rhythm patterns, set us off in a completely new direction – to find the joy in wanton destruction.

The Process

Each of the four actors were asked to create a simple eight-count gestural sequence, using only their hands, consisting of four imitations of the action select delete. To start with, these versions were to be fairly realistic, using notions of screens being wiped, disks being plucked and chucked, information being clutched and then vanishing into nothing. Once each performer had their eight, they were shared and learnt by everybody else. In order to ease the process, initial rehearsals used a different music track with a slightly slower tempo (Crazy P's 'Lady T – Hot Toddy Mix' for those who really want to get personal . . .). This stage took some time to learn. As with all challenges of this nature, it needs to become an exercise in muscle memory before it is possible to start playing with the detail and intention of the movement. On any given day, somebody who was incredibly confident with the material might suddenly

Finding the joy in wanton destruction: Cait Davis and Keir Charles rehearsing Select Delete in *pool (no water)*, 2006

fall apart. The non-progressive nature of exercises like this can sometimes lead to very frustrated cast members.

Once everybody was confident with the material we then set the cast the task of creating a foot pattern to accompany the material created for the hands. The instruction was to not move with every gesture but to pick out the more energetic gestural moves and move the body accordingly, freeing up the feet to side-step, shunt, step, pause – whatever the hands seemed to suggest. In making the feet and body correspond to the existing hands sequence, the entire movement vocabulary remained in the world of quick, neat, economic qualities that stayed in keeping with the music qualities we knew that 'Mic Check' would provide. One of the performers was also asked to create a further 16 Select Deletes which were to start pretty mundane but become more and more flamboyant as they progressed so that the hands began to operate with flair and, like a magician or card trickster, to defy logic and gravity. Selected objects might be flicked up into the air to remain there or tossed over shoulders or under armpits.

From here, the scene was a matter of structure and for this we turned entirely to the track we had chosen. We often find it inspiring to allow a music track to dictate structure, particularly when it is as challenging and original as something like 'Mic Check'. Of course there were elements within the text which suggested structural set-ups. To begin with, one character alone starts to select and delete, hence the solo of 16 movements he was asked to create. From there, the rest of the group are drawn into his actions as the movements become more and more extravagant. As the track began to fill out, so the entire group fell into a unison that itself became more and more effervescent. During a break in the track, the team also take a break, pinpointing images that remain, lining up for a final onslaught. Then, as the track reinstates itself, the group launch into the final onslaught, except this time the gestural sequence is at double speed and includes the feet and bodies material before a final coda that bursts into a whole new set of Select Deletes that sees the team now flinging their entire bodies into the air in jubilation.

The Development

In many ways, scenes such as this are very simple constructs. One area of development would be to experiment with the music track or count structure as it plays such an integral part in the scene if created in this way. For example, in 'Mic Check' there is a section of the track where there are nine descending notes followed by the first three of those nine notes being repeated twice. The whole structure is repeated four times. By numbering each note and then attaching a particular gesture to each of these numbers, the choreography is attributed a structure that is totally at the mercy of the music track in terms of tempo and incidence. By listening to the note structure of any particular track it would be interesting to tie movements to notes or even phrases and to see what choreographic results emerge.

This type of creative exercise might also be useful in the early stages of combining text with movement. Any two words might be used. A binary opposition would be a good starting point.

Exhaustion   *Klub 1995*

The Idea

Exhaustion was the final scene in *Klub*, a physical sequence that played with both the notion and the practice of exhaustion. This came from observations and experiences in clubs where the levels of physical energy and endurance – all in the name of a good time – seemed both inspirational and extreme.

The Process

The piece was created in the summer of 1995 with the UK rave scene still enjoying spectacular success, notoriety and media coverage. Manchester's Hacienda had yet to close its doors. There was the much publicised death of Leah Betts after taking ecstacy and collapsing. 'Club culture' was a legitimate area of social study, not just on the covers of the tabloids but within credible publications such as *Rave Off*. Against this backdrop, *Klub* was our take on the hysterical depiction of this 'underground' practice – although it was always hard to understand how paying £15 entry fees and £4 for a bottle of water constituted acts that ever felt truly 'underground' for anyone.

The first idea for the scene was to create a physical sequence that would simply move from the back of the performing space to the very front with a timing of approximately three and a half minutes – the average length of a radio edit club track at the time. This got spiked before we even broke out in a sweat over it. The term 'In Yer Face' theatre was already very popular at that time and it was felt that, even looking at it diagrammatically in our notebooks, the idea was in danger of being 'In Yer Face' made terribly real. Another consideration was the tour the piece would have to embark upon, taking in a vast range of different-sized spaces. Some of these would provide so little depth that the idea of using such a spatial dynamic to create all the tension for the final scene would be virtually impossible in certain venues. Either that or the scene would run for 18 seconds in such spaces.

The next development looked at literally throwing each other along a line. *Klub* featured six performers and such numbers made it physically possible to create a genuine 'line' of people rather than the casual gathering afforded by three people waiting to catch a fourth. The idea also tied in with physical sequences already in place within the show reflecting the idea of the assembly line. Whereas these earlier scenes played with the notions of rigidity, constriction and confinement, the idea here was to go for physical abandonment, risk and flight. An early version of this seemed to be getting us somewhere and was held for a while. Returning to the section towards the end of the six-week rehearsals we found ourselves to be a company covered in bruises. Aching, tired and made immediately angry on attempting the physical work (rolling over bruised limbs continuously), we were very different people. *Klub* felt like a very brutal experience and Exhaustion suddenly needed to fulfil much more. Maybe it was a desire to really serve the piece we had just made or maybe it was a last ditch attempt to show *Klub* that we were hard enough to take it on. Whatever our motives, it became apparent that the levels at which you can jump at somebody or be caught by somebody were rather limited. Trying to jump *harder* at someone proved difficult enough. Trying to *catch someone* harder, impossible. We were also eager to create something that allowed us the freedom to continuously push its boundaries as a movement sequence. The initial *Klub* tour was long and we needed a scene that allowed us to break our own physical limits again and again and again.

A late night rehearsal (as always) cracked it. A discussion about the brutal nature of dancing in some of the harder techno clubs and a decision to base the scene around this with added keywords 'fear' and 'adrenalin' saw us start to work on a sequence.

In pairs we worked on falling to the floor – only with the added thrill of doing it as fast as we could. The 'faller' had to act with speed and rigidity and the 'catcher' had no time to think about anything at all really. What immediately excited us was the way in which there was no time for technique. This didn't mean that the whole thing looked messy. On the contrary, catches within the sequence were often the most graceful physical union of two beings ever seen on a Frantic stage. These were matched in their beauty only by the sheer brutality of those desperate car crash saves that also littered the sequence. Running this version a number of times revealed the consistency of inconsistency within the scene.

Taking the track 'Access' (DJ Misjah) as our structure we began to set the sequence. 'Access' is a gloriously hard techno track that contains one of the finest builds in dance music. From this we literally built the risk on stage over the next three minutes. In our notebooks, the notation looked something like this:

F1 (Stack) M1 (Catch)

F1 (Stack) M1 (Catch) enter F2 (Stack)

F1 (Stack) M1 (Catch) F2 (Stack) M2 (Catch)

F1 (Catch) M1 (Stack) F2 (Catch) M2 (Stack) F3 (Catch) M3 (Stack)

To 'stack' was our term for falling and the development of the sequence started from one lone female performer (F1) running at full speed in the space and choosing a moment to 'stack' at which point a male performer (M1) appears and catches her (mostly). The appearance of a second female performer at full speed created certain obvious problems for the male performer until the high speed arrival of a second male performer. The following arrival of a third male performer sees the shift of risk as the female performers then become responsible for catching men falling at speed.

For us, this part of the scene encapsulated the notion of the collective energy and recklessness so evident on Britain's dancefloors. A wild abandonment with seemingly no notion of safety, driven by something close to a sonic battering. From here we then wanted to move internally but without losing any of the energy already in the space. Asked what kind of movement might possibly be the next step, our choreographer Stephen Kirkham replied 'Stack . . .'

The result became something of a Frantic landmark, where the now solo performers threw themselves into the air as high as possible then landed with no technique, only the desire to create a scene of sheer physical excess; an attempt to push our physical endurance and to try to match the sheer might of the now pounding track (depending on the speaker systems in each venue, admittedly). Exhaustion earned its title and the resultant scene suddenly felt like the perfect ending if an ending, is to be defined as the point from which there is nowhere else to go, nothing more to offer, no energy left to give, and from which we dare go no further.

The Development

For the reasons mentioned above we are going to make no bones about ducking out of this one and handing it over to you. Good luck!

chapter three

Playing with scenes

We hope that the preceding examples inspire you to play with process. We must stress again that it is the process that is going to be of most use to you.

The following scenes either went through various transitions while still in rehearsal, or have been adapted by us from their initial production to serve a different production. This chapter is still about **The Idea** and **The Process**, but this time it is specifically about *our* **Development** of the process.

Lovebench   *Klub 1996*

Lovebench is a scene inspired by the idea of a society where genuine contact is becoming harder to find. It is about the fear of failing in that search, of trashing the fragile moment before contact. It is moments full of hope and possibility of fulfilment yet it is destined for failure. Every tiny attempt to make contact is a step on the moon.

The setting was a simple bench, or rather two small benches stacked to make a higher bench. The cast were split into pairs and those pairs were numbered groups 1 to 3. In these pairs we improvised moments where, not looking at each other, we would try to make intimate contact, i.e. a hand caress, an arm around the shoulder, fingers across face. Even though both partners may want to make contact, their nervous actions are working against each other so that contact becomes impossible and the moment is ultimately lost. To further complicate things, one of the partners has a small stereo in their hands. This stereo provides the actual soundtrack to the scene (poor quality, tinny, batteries fading – we also used a version of 'Love is Strange' performed by Everything But The Girl). The stereo is often exchanged in the confusion, its journey very much part of the choreography.

When each couple has a small string of material ending with one of them leaving we then start to put the whole cast's work together. Group 1 may start and once they finish with one of them still on the bench they are then joined by one of the performers from group 2. These two performers create a short 'crossover' section where they may or may not be aware of each other. Through this the stereo gets exchanged and the last performer from group 1 leaves and is replaced by the second performer from group 2. They then go through their prepared section. At the end one of them leaves and the first performer from group 3 joins and creates a crossover section with the remaining performer from group 2, ultimately being joined by their partner to perform their prepared section as group 3.

This is the basic form. From here we can take an outside eye to see whether it is working in this format, whether the pairings work, whether the 'stories' are clear, and whether there is more to be squeezed from this choreography. In performance this scene was a bit more complicated than the initial process outlined above. Certain pairings may have returned, but this time their story had stopped being funny and had become tragic, and vice versa.

To complement and contrast with this physical tale of tragic misfortune in the search for love we created another scene very much inspired by that quest but much more from the hedonistic world of *Klub*. Lovebench 2 was a reprise in theory but it was the previous world exploded. It is brash and committed and debauched. It does not care for etiquette. It crashes, gropes and fondles its way towards contact and fulfilment. It is casual and reckless and does not fear failure. The physicality is a million miles away from Lovebench 1 (as is the music used) but it is directly inspired by it. It is a nihilistic and cynical response to the mannered world of Lovebench 1.

In Lovebench 2 the two small benches were separated and placed alongside each other. Performers would burst into the space with much more confidence and energy and, dressed provocatively, launch themselves at the benches, which quickly became podiums. From these podiums the characters would leer and flaunt themselves as shamelessly and aggressively as the *Klub* environment would let them. This is sex driven and fearless of failure, in stark contrast to the timid courtship of Lovebench 1. Performers would leap across and onto the benches, make lunges towards each other and throw themselves suggestively into the arms of their partners. Where the hands or eyes of partners would nearly meet in Lovebench 1, here they were allowed to devour each other. Where there was excitement and hope in an apparently accidental caress in Lovebench 1, here there appeared to be only instant gratification – that is, if the characters were ever able to stop posturing and gyrating and make lasting, meaningful contact. This is a self-obsessed world.

As this choreography of highly physical and fleeting sexual encounters continues it becomes less about couples and more about individuals claiming their per-ceived right to behave in this way. Once again the existence of Lovebench 1 serves to undermine this slightly hollow victory, as we have earlier seen the same characters on a much different quest. Opposing the two Lovebench scenes offered a balanced view we did not initially anticipate being able to achieve, as it was the creation of Lovebench 1 that made it possible to create Lovebench 2. Without the first world the second world would have no resonance and vice versa. They both played on the desire for intimacy and contact even if they presented very different worlds. They were able to comment on each other as two approaches towards this same intimacy and contact.

To create Lovebench 2 we required a fair amount of physical dexterity and energy. In performance it was one of the most tiring scenes of a very tiring show and certainly resulted in the most cuts and bruises. At its heart, though, is the extreme posturing of sexual courtship. That posturing is focused initially inward towards other characters and then it seeks out the audience. Couples would make small sections of work based on this extreme flirting and then they would replace each other quickly on the podium. As the pace was increased so was the intensity of the interaction, with couples working on short, stylised and highly physical sections, moving and throwing each other around and onto the podiums. From here the relationship breaks down as they are all overtaken by the need to present themselves not to their partners but to the largest possible audience. The focus shifts out beyond the fourth wall.

(It is useful to remember the stages of creation behind these scenes so that they can be informative and useful to you in your physical devising.)

The initial idea was the need and desire for contact and intimacy. From deciding on a simple setting we created equally simple choreography, clearly aiming for contact and intimacy within that setting. (A park bench?) A piece of music was chosen that complemented and invoked the world we were aiming for.

From here we recognised the need to complement and contrast this world. We set about making a new scene inspired by and true to the structure of the first scene – complete with intimacy, contact, near misses, sex/love. We then identified that the new world had to be brash where the first world was well mannered and this had to be portrayed through every aspect of the scene, from its physicality to its costume and the music employed.

These were the simple rules. It is possible to follow these rules and create a completely different set of scenes from ours. And if your starting point is not about the need and desire for contact and intimacy and about something different, e.g. the mistrust of strangers, then you could use every stage to create two opposing and complementary scenes. One could be fuelled by notions of how we would like to embrace strangers yet still hold a quiet suspicion of them and the second could be about all-out xenophobia and paranoia. The reason that they may still work is because they might still comment on each other, i.e. the brazen, if unpleasant, honesty of the second section may show up a slightly dishonest, underhand attitude in the seemingly benign first section.

Guyscrapers   *Hymns 1999*

(We admit Guyscrapers is a very cheesy name for the scene, but you will understand why it is called that when you read on!)

Most of the scenes in this chapter have been enhanced by some kind of physical devising process. We set out to crack this scene in much the same way but right from the start we were flailing and failing. It is included here because of the simplicity of what we learnt in the making of it. It does not follow the Idea/Process/Development structure of the previous scenes because we feel that it is very obvious what the lesson to be learnt from this is and it is completely subjective.

This is probably the simplest scene in the show *Hymns*. Characters Scott and Steven grab a quiet moment following the turmoil of an explosive physical scene. What follows is a gentle scene where Steven tries to engage with his once close friend but finds that time and their mixed feelings over their friend's death have had a corrosive effect.

We talked with *Hymns* writer Chris O'Connell about how we wanted this to be an 'empty' scene, for the silences to scream out. We had to see the effort it takes these guys to speak in this moment. We needed to see the risk associated with them sharing their feelings. If we are to feel the pain of two close friends being so guarded, then we must appreciate their fear of falling versus their desire to connect.

We considered various approaches to achieving this, including some complex choreography running under the scene to betray the fear and desperation at the situation. It was then that we realised that we were becoming guilty of crowding the scene, of cluttering it with moves that bombard the audience with the supposedly subtle subtext. A much simpler route was taken and it was one that showed much more faith in the performers and in the text.

This was a very important lesson for us, one that we had been stressing to other practitioners and yet were in danger of ignoring ourselves. Simply, we were dancing all over a text that we had specifically asked to be sparse and brittle, forgetting those inherent qualities and not allowing the knowledge and understanding of the performers to carry the scene.

Once the performers were allowed to play with the scene, keeping it as simple as possible and letting the silences speak out, it became clear how physicality could enhance the performance of this section. Director Liam Steel realised that the physical situation of the characters could have a massive impact on the playing and reading of the scene. Their physical situation had to reflect their emotional situation. Here were two old friends having a quiet moment after their mate's funeral but all is not well. They are struggling to connect again and there is obviously an undercurrent to their stilted conversation. Both men are emotionally out of their comfort zones. The decision was made to take the performers/characters out of their physical comfort zones too.

They both took chairs and placed them at the top of one of the ladders that comprised the set. They sat close together but crucially not facing each other. The sheer height at which the flimsy-looking metal chairs were placed (with custom-made hooks on the back for this very purpose of attaching them to the ladders) meant that the physical setting of the scene created a feeling of danger. The performers are in a physically dangerous place just as their characters are in an emotionally dangerous place. This affects the way the audience watch the scene. They subliminally gain an understanding of the risk involved for the characters. Physically and metaphorically, one slip (of the tongue) and they are in trouble.

The simplicity of this scene has always made it stand out. It is important to remember that an interest in the physical side of theatre is not an exclusively binding commitment to interpret every scene physically. Even though the success of this scene is partly due to its physical interpretation, the process or journey to its ultimate presentation involved us recognising that we were trying to do too much to the scene and were effectively smothering it. It is not good enough to throw 'physical theatre' at a scene because we are a 'physical' theatre company.

What we also found was that Guyscrapers presented a massive change in focus. From the spectacle of the previously highly physical scenes, the audience are now asked to look at a very still, naturalistic scene. It is this change of focus, we believe, that keeps audiences fresh. There is no point following a big physical scene with another big physical scene. They cancel each other out.

A friend observed that a rule of thumb used in film is that a shot must change by 30 percent from the preceding shot if it is to be seen to be effective and keep the viewer interested. We feel this is a very good rule to observe in theatre too.

Stockholm Fight   *Stockholm 2007*

Stockholm Fight is a slightly special case in this chapter. The process used is a good example of allowing a physical quality to permeate a production as it actually created three separate physical scenes.

This is not here just as an exercise in economy but it also serves to show how the meaning of choreography lies in the context in which it is presented. We have used the same or similar choreography to show the unravelling of a relationship over one intense night. This process is similar to the approach used by a soundtrack composer on a film, creating motifs and variations on a theme to highlight different levels of tension. Sometimes the music is familiar and comforting. At other times it makes us nervous and fearful.

The tension in *Stockholm* built up to a brutal and shocking fight between a couple who had charmed us and sold us a vision of their perfect life together. All their defences drop as they shatter in front of us. The intention was that these people would feel like our friends and while we are shocked and appalled by the nature of their destruction, there is still part of us that understands why they will forever crawl back to each other.

We approached the making of the fight in a roundabout way. We did not engage the performers in any violent choreographic tasks. We wanted the violence to come from somewhere deep in their relationship and we did not

Georgina Lamb and Samuel James in love and at war in *Stockholm*, 2007

want the violence to completely overshadow the love at the heart of this relationship.

There is a further complexity in that these are two people who love each other, yet frustrate each other. It is the quest for annihilation on one side and the denial of violence on the other. It is not all-out war. There are different dynamics at work in there.

There were two major devising tasks that went into this scene:

1 Their Dance

This initial work was part of the research and development sessions and then carried into the rehearsals proper.

We set the performers the task of creating a beautiful and graceful dance routine bordering on ballroom and tango. We wanted them to possess a physicality that might not have been seen in previous Frantic shows. None of us were trained in those techniques so we were really looking at approximations. Being avid avoiders of any Saturday night celebrity dance competitions we aspired to develop a hybrid style of movement that could look genuine but was not necessarily stuck in any one style. The point was not that they were a certain type of dancer, just that they loved to dance. It was to be beautiful. We wanted this dance to be a major part of how they expressed their love and joy for each other. We wanted it to charm us and make us want to be them.

Once we had made this string of tango-esque material we then created different contexts in which the performers could dance.

1   While dancing they had to say sorry to each other when it felt right. They had to keep saying sorry and build in intensity throughout. The results were very striking. The raw passion was amazing but it was never a simple presentation of increasing remorse. Sometimes the 'sorry' became very aggressive, the hold on the partner appeared to become crushing and the whole tone of the piece had changed from joyful to heartbreaking or terrifying.
2   Again, keeping the same moves, they entered another scenario. We created a room using an old metal filing cabinet, tables and chairs and placed plastic bottles and knives and forks precariously around the place. The room was made as small as possible. Claustrophobic and cramped.

The performers were asked to commit to the set moves. These moves required a much bigger space and would lead to the performers clattering into the furniture and knocking over the bottles and cutlery. They had to ignore the chaos they were creating and keep dancing.

What transpired was a couple oblivious to the end of the world. Or was this a couple causing the end of the world? Did their love transcend this chaos or was it the root of it?

3   This time we arranged a room of tables and chairs. It was set out roughly like a kitchen with lots of worktop surfaces. Again the performers were to stick to their choreography where possible but it was all to happen off the floor, across the tables and chairs.

Here the moves quickly became dangerous. They also became a challenge and a ritual between two people as they tested each other's commitment, careering across gaps and teetering on precipices.

The three scenarios above brought out a lot of the potential in the movement. The interesting thing to note was that it was the setting or theatrical context that was crucial to this potential meaning rather than the choreography itself. The moves ultimately bent under the weight of the context, but the joy of seeing them exist in one context and then struggling to exist again in another was fascinating.

The beauty of Their Dance was an important part of the portrayal of the couple in *Stockholm*. It was crucial to get this right, to suggest the couple were capable of such beauty as well as the carnage of their later scenes. It was this dichotomy that gives them depth as a couple and makes their predicament painful and tragic. We never wanted to dismiss this couple as just hateful and violent.

The exercises opened some interesting possibilities about how we could use Their Dance. Once we had achieved the beauty it was extremely useful to see how dark and disturbing the same choreography could become through a change in context. The dance moves could then become motifs and pliable to the retrograde and expansion employed by any dance company worth their leg warmers.

This extract from one of our notebooks shows how the dance was already becoming a vital part of the storytelling:

Does the dance break down?
Does it become exhausting?
A ritual? A symbolic act?

Bullying? A reluctant partner?
Is it performed in increasingly smaller spaces? On a podium?
Dangerous? Perilous?
Risk – To stop is to fall off – metaphor
Along the top of the kitchen?
A desperate, exhausted act . . .
Or a passionate act of apology . . .
An attempt to recapture something?
A definition of their relationship that bears less relation to reality the more they do it? e.g. Man leads – woman follows, but outside the dance he is losing all power?

2 Push and Pull

Recognising the many dynamics that exist and conflict in this complex relationship, we set the performers off on a simple choreographic task. (Remember, we have not told them that this has anything to do with the fight or their characters.)

Using Round/By/Through (page 131) as a base (a technique inspired by the title words of the exercise), we asked them to create a string of material exploring the transference of control which had a push–pull quality. This would mean moving their partner but stopping them before the move is complete, e.g. pushing away but suddenly stopping them; pulling them and then blocking them. They had to try smaller moves too, e.g. throwing a partner's hand up and then stopping it dead.

The exercise was simply about push and pull, start and stop, but the control would constantly swap back and forward between partners after a few moves.

As this was billed as an exploratory exercise, it meant it escaped any declamatory and 'fighty' quality. It was just a sometimes simple, sometimes intricate exchange of manipulation and control. One partner would provoke the other into a move but would stop the move before completion, as if to emphasise their control. They might push their partner away and almost instantly pull their partner back under their control.

Once the choreography was secure we could test it through slight directorial adjustments, just as we had done with Their Dance, to see what more it could offer us. First we brutalised it. The performers could use more force and speed but had to retain the precision. Their touch would press harder and deeper into their partner's body. Then we stripped it of all the sharp and confrontational quality and softened the moves. This became a very tender and playful string of material (more on this below).

We now had a wide range of complex physicality to draw on. We used some of the moves from the 'dance' and then arrested them with the 'push–pull' material. We wanted the fight to have this depth and physicality and felt that it would not have been possible to have shades of love mixed with the struggle for power if we had simply approached the scene with the intention of making a standard fight.

That said, it had to be brutal and we worked hard on this quality once the performers were comfortable with the choreography. If we had worked on the scrappiness of it too early, it would only ever have been scrappy. By taking something secure and at times beautiful and then making it scrappy, we were able to retain and hint at some of its former quality. This is literally what we wanted the fight to do – present something brutal that suggests a connection to something beautiful.

The final stage was to take the choreography, all of which had been made off the set, and put it onto the set. We used the same route around the kitchen as Their Dance and then embraced any moments the set itself offered. By placing it in its context we could make the adjustments necessary to ensure we were not just expressing the fight through dance. It had to feel just like a fight but have the heightened physicality of dance. Placing it on the set was the last step in making it real.

A by-product of this approach was the creation of the Tea Towels scene. Midway through the process we explored a tender and playful version of the choreography. We took this quality and improvised with it.

This quality actually first surfaced during the development workshops. Here we gave the performers tea towels and got them to tidy up the kitchen while still committing to the choreography. At times the top half of the body was busy denying the existence of the choreography while the bottom half was playing out. At other times the performers were moving each other around the room with a matter-of-fact physicality.

We played with the potential of this. Could the couple use the moves to make up? To say sorry? To say I am still pissed off with you? To say you don't get round me that easily?

What emerged looked like a semi-willing game. It had a complex sexiness to it as one partner would submit to the physical commands of the other and then instantly switch to dominance. We got them to try to make each other laugh during it as the intensity built, or whisper something to each other.

Again the journey matched that of Their Dance. The finished scene was a charming game of cat and mouse, of trying to apologise and trying not to be put off by the other person. It was a lovely scene where one tried to resist the other working their magic upon them and failed miserably and beautifully. It was joyous to watch.

That did not save it from being cut though! The scene destroyed the rhythm of the show and had to be excised. Here was a scene born from a pseudo ballroom/tango dance and the desire to create a complex and terrifying fight. It contained many of the moves and most of the same journey but it was a million miles from either scene.

The thing to take from this is the simplicity of the processes (Their Dance, Push and Pull) and the potential they have to keep offering more and more meaning.

part two
practical exercises

chapter four

Getting started

Initial movement sessions

In the early stages of rehearsal we may ask our performers to improvise using rolls and lifts without ever coming off the floor. Smooth contact work looks at taking the effort and conflict out of physical contact. They are instructed to continually move across the floor taking each other's weight and momentum, 'listening' to their partner's physicality and learning how their partners operate. This stands the performers in good stead for when they have to work quickly together to make material for the show. These initial sessions are all about opportunities and possibilities.

This is also a development towards a strong, grounded performance quality and to make sure there is never an element of 'waft' in the physicality. It is not full of meaning or emotion at this stage. The performers are working very hard to explore and retain a particular truthful quality.

When setting up a session like this, always look out for students/performers overly emoting during movement, embellishing their moves with earth shattering importance. It is important to aim for something more naturalistic. Movement can be a heightened reality and can be rooted in everyday situations and, most poignantly, be performed by everyday characters. Encourage your performers to use their personalities within movement and not to lose themselves behind a physical theatre mask. Allowing your own personality to come through moves is the first step to allowing your adopted character's personality to be expressed and developed through movement.

Trust

A massive part in creating a conducive environment for producing good work is achieving trust. This should be a major priority.

This is NOT about ingratiating yourself.

This is NOT about dated and cringeworthy trust games.

This is NOT about telling your participants your deepest and darkest secrets within the first 20 minutes of meeting them.

This is NOT about plying them with cake and biscuits.

It is NOT about being everyone's best mate.

This IS about breaking down inhibitions.

This IS about setting high standards and keeping to them.

This IS about leading but also listening.

This IS about reading body language and group dynamics.

This IS about having a plan yet being prepared to throw it away.

This IS about motivating, encouraging and praising where necessary.

We have always found that people can do more than they think they can. They can be pushed to surprise themselves. But you cannot just expect someone to fly without giving them flying lessons. Confidence and trust go hand in hand and should be worked at.

The importance of rules, time frames and limitations

The little details – owning the space

A conducive environment for your participants is more than a creative process. It is a first impression when they walk in the room. It is the temperature, the smell, the lighting and the music playing. It is the atmosphere. You can go a long way to dictating the mood and success of the session through controlling that first impression.

Jimmy Akingbola and Claire-Louise Cordwell as Othello and Desdemona, *Othello* rehearsals © Manuel Harlan

Pushing it a little – you are the boss

We have found that people produce their best work when they are hot and sweaty through exertion, when they are focused and committed. This, of course, creates a hot and sweaty room. Wherever possible resist the temptation to throw open all the doors and windows, the fire escapes, to let the fresh air in. Believe us, something more valuable will escape! As soon as the outside world crashes in with its noises and smells, the world you have created dissolves. The focus is gone.

Give breaks when needed. Look out for exhausted participants. Put their welfare first. But don't submit to the first request, for they do not always know what they are losing. When we deny requests for the window to be opened we always explain exactly what we will lose and we have never had any complaints. It helps to explain the dangers of warm muscles cooling down rapidly and then being asked to move again. There is real risk of injury here.

Improvisation rules

Of course some rules are there to be broken, but so far we've preferred to stick to the 'one track' rule when improvising.

The 'one track' rule came about when we realised that we could remember nothing from the endless physical improvisation we had just been through. It had felt great and we were sure there had been some wonderful moments, but there was no way we could detail them. So the 'one track' rule limited the improvisation to the length of the music used to accompany the exercise.

This was symptomatic of the way we worked back then. Being in the shows and trying to direct and/or choreograph is a difficult situation. We are not in the shows any more and the use of the video camera in the rehearsal room has softened the rule slightly, but we feel it still serves us well in the rehearsal room. It stops improvisations becoming indulgent and allows us to quickly get our heads together, find out what we all have learnt and try it again or something new.

The structure of the week in rehearsals

This is something we have come across very lately and it has been 'acquired' from the Australian Dance Theatre. It is common sense really but it has shaped the rehearsal process for our last few shows.

We now make sure that we work our performers hard, physically, for only two days in a row. The third day is for recuperation and will be focused on text or gentle physicality. The 'two days on, one day off' rule helps you structure your rehearsals in advance, with your performers' welfare in mind. And you will hopefully not be surprised or obstructed by tired performers.

This is the basic structure of the week. You can also structure each day in advance. We start every day with a warm-up (even the calm third day). Physical work dominates the morning and text tends to dominate the afternoon. Immediately after lunch we play a game to sharpen, engage and enthuse our performers. Too many afternoons have been scuppered by the post-carb collapse. Rehearsing in the afternoon can feel like hard work, especially if the muscles have cooled down over lunch and the lactic acid has started to build up. A fun game can be 20 minutes well spent if it gets everyone active and alert again.

Morning warm-ups – teamwork and personal attainment

Warm-ups should be tailored to what you are about to do. For example, lift work requires specific attention to the performers' backs; count-based choreography can be eased into through games like Quad.

Warm-ups are also a good time to build up a team mentality and concentrate on building strength and setting goals. Press-ups, sit-ups and Pilates can all start at an easy and manageable level but we feel it is crucial to raise the number the next day. One more press-up is progress. It is really useful to have your cast achieve something new and better than they have before, to keep raising their level of attainment each morning. Even if it is only press-ups. It charts an improvement and it is also a promise of what we are going to achieve together. If we do 10 press-ups on day one of a 25-day rehearsal period, then you are promising them that they *will* get to a level where they will be capable of doing 35 press-ups on the last day.

Similar useful attainment target exercises include holding a handstand against a wall for, say, 30 seconds. It is an excellent upper body strength exercise.

It is good to do this in pairs so that while one is doing the handstand, the other is keeping their partner secure and is there for them if they think they are going to fall. Most importantly, they are there to give encouragement throughout. This relationship is reciprocated when they swap over.

Not everyone will be able to stay in the handstand for the whole time. This is fine. Simply ask them to remember exactly how long they lasted (you can shout the time every five seconds) and this becomes their target to beat next time.

This rule applies across the board. If you fall short of the group target, then all you have to do is attack your own personal record. Commitment to improvement is all we ask (demand!).

Always forward, never backwards

This is such a simple mantra but it has been so useful in all aspects of our work. Specifically with young groups it is expressed as our company maxim, our commitment to always striving to do something better than before.

Young groups may be suitably fascinated by a creative devising process, but the repetition and polishing needed to make any scene ready for performance might be a new demand upon them. It can also feel dull and unrewarding when all they want to do is work on new things.

By applying the maxim to the rehearsal the targets are clear. It must be smoother than before. Or faster than before. Or cleaner than before.

It may not seem very theatrical, but if you need a physical scene to speed up to match the perfect piece of music, then share that information with the cast. Get the stopwatch out. The goal of the perfect timing becomes clear, shared and attainable. The maxim makes it clear from the outset that you will not settle for anything less than improvement each time.

Residencies

We have talked about the need for a conducive environment. One of the main challenges that faced us when we led residencies in schools was replicating that environment. (Residencies are usually a week-long intensive session, full time with the same group, culminating in a public performance of an original devised production.)

Institutions are, of course, institutionalised. When the school bell rings, that Pavlovian response kicks in and people reach for their bags. With the permission of the school or department within it we sought to fight that. We created a working environment where we would give people exactly the breaks that they were entitled to but at a time that was convenient for us, or they would be scheduled to fit in with the requirements of the production. This helped to instil the work ethic we needed from the participants.

The reasoning behind this was that we wanted to turn our participants into a professional company for the week. We wanted them to care passionately about the outcome of this production and to spur each other on to achieve the best they could.

For the week, they were members of Frantic Assembly and we let it be known to them that we were not going to let this production damage our reputation. It meant that they were doing it for themselves and they were doing it for us. For the week, we were treating them as professional performers and with that came the demands and the rewards. As a group we would decide on a company name and then actively market the company and the show to the public. We would never talk about the performance being seen by mums and dads but by the paying public. And the paying public would demand value.

All of this creates pressure but also a focus. It pays to set a target and to let people know that you not only have these high expectations but believe in the ability of your participants to fulfil those expectations. Our experience in working with young people on devising projects is that the real limitations are the self-perceived limitations. Everybody reacts well to achieving something they thought they could not. We always set our target just beyond this self-perceived limitation.

SUGGESTIONS FOR CONSTRUCTIVE WARM-UPS

These exercises are useful in creating a more relaxed and fluid physicality. They do not replace more formal stretches, especially if the group are about to embark on some strenuous lifting, but they can play a crucial part in introducing the group to very important concepts needed in the more energetic work. They are very important building blocks that can and should be referred to in the creative choreographic processes.

Rolling 1 and 2, as you will see, are relevant to contact processes like Round/ By/Through. Push Hands is usually our first building block before embarking on any lifting choreography.

These exercises are both warm-ups and fundamental training processes.

Rolling 1

This is a seemingly very simple exercise that is well worth taking the time to get right. Principally it is rolling across the floor, but there are very specific rules and instructions that lead the participant to a much better understanding of how their body moves.

It is also a gentle way into much more vigorous exercises.

Start by asking for a volunteer. It is very important that the group are observing each other as the success or failure of the following tasks is instantly visible.

Ask the volunteer to lie on their back with their hands above their head at one end of the room. You are going to get them to demonstrate rolling down the room. (You are going to manhandle them here. It might be best to warn them and make sure they are OK with this. What you are actually about to demonstrate is a moving technique similar to that used by nurses when turning over a patient.)

Crouch by the side of your volunteer making sure that you are on the side leading into the room. Ask your volunteer to raise their knee furthest away from you. Their feet should still be on the floor. There should be no effort here; the key is to stay relaxed.

Place your hand on the raised knee and quickly but gently pull it towards you, across their body. This will turn the volunteer over onto their front. Make sure you guide the knee to facilitate this.

A successful demonstration of this technique will show your observers how easily the body can be moved. Now ask your volunteer to replicate this move. Place your hand on their knee but do not pull. They must relax but just allow their knee to move towards the warmth of your hand. Again, if this is successful, you will see how the body leads with the knee, twists and allows the rest of the body to follow in a logical order until gravity takes over and completes the turn. This twist should be obvious to the observers. It looks like a ripple that runs up the body, meaning that the head is the last body part to complete the turn.

The next stage is harder but importantly works on exactly the same principle.

Your volunteer is now lying on their front. (Remind them to keep their arms above their head. They do not want them to get caught up in the rolling of the body.) Place your hand on the back of their head. They are to move their head towards the hand. The hand should lead them back onto their front by gently pulling away and across the body, just as you did with the knee. What makes it more difficult is that the volunteer will encounter a block. The head will feel that it cannot go any further, that they are stretching as far as they can. This is where you have to remind them of the natural logic we found in the first roll. Simply get them to have a think about this logic and consider the next part of their body that needs to follow the head. It is their shoulder. Is it relaxed? Once it is relaxed can it follow the head and send the ripple down the body from shoulder to hips, to knees, to feet?

Participants should always be on the look-out for this logic. They will encounter moments where they will feel stuck and will say they are stuck. Sometimes it is enough to remind them of the logic and they can release themselves.

Now it is time to put both rolls together. Get the volunteer to imagine the need to move across the room to the other side. This is the only motivation. The rules are that the body is being led by, alternately, the knee and the head. The volunteer also has to be encouraged to think about the next move just before the current move ends. This provides a fluid transition. Observers can see the ripple running up and down the body. (It might help to get the rollers to imagine the room is tipping away from them, assisting their roll.)

Be on the look-out for rollers getting carried away and rushing it. Rollers need to keep thinking throughout the exercise to achieve the ripple! When they get too fast you will notice that participants are rolling their hips. This mostly happens when they are trying to roll from their front to their back, leading with their head. If this is happening, then slow them down and place a hand on the small of their back and then their stomach to remind them that the middle of their body should be following and not leading. It moves when it logically needs to.

You can set the whole group off, taking turns, in twos, at rolling across the room. Encourage those waiting to look out for that successful ripple up and down the body.

Once you are happy that your group have got this principle then you may instruct them to try a freestyle run! In this they choose a clear body part to lead the roll. They should aim for the same smooth and fluid transitions and their choice of body part should be instantly apparent to any observers.

See how fast they can go while retaining the quality of movement. Never be afraid to remind the participants of the simplest form of this activity – the first building block, the knee and the head – if clarity and quality begin to be compromised.

You can return to this type of movement and start to play. Maybe the choice of body part could take them up from the floor briefly. Try placing obstacles in the way of the simple journey. How do they interact with these? Can they find a way of getting in and out of a chair placed somewhere en route and still maintain the fluidity and logic of the original task? Try placing other participants in their way, kneeling down, lying down, etc. These could be moving platforms to negotiate, but participants should understand that they are fleeting moments as the simple drive of getting across the room must not be forgotten.

This task is not just about helping people find a fluid way to roll across the floor. We sometimes use this exercise as a way into much more complex contact partner work. There are moments in such complex exercises where participants find themselves talking about being 'stuck' and unable to find a way out of a move. The rolling exercise is a good reference point for moments like this. Knowing how to continue with the flow of a move or using different body parts to lead can really help when creating contact work.

You can apply the logic you have found in the rolling to contact work. The rolling exercise is a good reminder of how someone can be active in a move even if they are being lifted. All it takes is to think about the exercise for a moment and apply a physical logic to the situation. The slight twist of the hips or turn of the head can open up loads of new possibilities for a dueting couple.

There is an interesting development to this rolling exercise. It uses alternate focuses of head/armpit and knee.

Ifan Meredith in rehearsal for *Frankenstein*, 2008

Use a volunteer couple. Get one of them to lie on the floor (A) and get the other (B) to stand above them. The one on the floor has to respond to the contact from the partner standing up. B has to lift or push the prone partner using their feet. They place their foot under A's knee and kick (push) it so that A rolls over onto their front with their arms above their head. Then B puts their foot under A's armpit and does the same so that A flips over onto their back, taking the impulse from the foot into the armpit and sending it spiralling down the body as they roll over. Repeat this making sure that A is still taking B's impetus and is not just rolling. With a bit of practice and an increase in speed and fluidity, the effect is of someone kicking another, rag doll like, across the stage. This can be quite a dramatic and startling effect.

Rolling 2

We have talked at length about the simple rolling exercises and their relevance to creating contact partner work while stood. This next exercise uses rolling but, building on the variation at the end of Rolling 1, solely involves working in pairs on the floor. We will also talk later about the 'log' and the 'rock' – two devices that help practitioners to visualise the kind of rolling movement they should be aiming for.

Ideally make sure your volunteer couple are of similar weight or build for this exercise. (It would be even better if you could demonstrate this exercise with someone.)

Both volunteers lie on the floor next to each other. They should start with their heads facing the same way and their arms above their heads. This time they do not have to think about individual body parts. They can roll in any way.

Make sure they are touching and ask them to roll the same way while maintaining this friction.

The person at the back needs to be thinking about this contact and this friction as they move across the room. They can use their arm, leg or head to make contact with such weight that they 'stick' to their partner and start to move over them. They need to concentrate on merely pressing down and not think about trying to roll over their partner. The effect we are looking for will not be achieved if the person moving over is actually trying to move themselves or throw their body over their partner's. They have to stick to the simplicity of the task and just let the move happen.

This successful connection through friction is sometimes called the 'hook'. Unfortunately this is misleading because if you were to actually hook onto your partner, then you would be liable to trap your arm under your partner as you both roll. You would also drop to the floor as you fall off your partner.

The person at the front just keeps rolling. The lifting is purely a consequence of their rolling. They will have to work hard on keeping the roll going with their partner's weight on them. As they roll, if a good connection is made, their partner will be rolled over their body. Think of the way ancient civilisations are believed to have moved large rocks by rolling logs underneath them. In both cases the item/person being moved remains passive. It just offers its constant weight.

When the person moving gets to the other side of their partner they smoothly make the transition from 'rock' to 'log' and continue the rolling momentum. As this happens the first 'log' needs to switch mindset to become the 'rock' and look for connections through friction (or hook). A successful couple can make several fluid transitions across the room.

There is always a chance that the transition will not happen straightaway, but it is better for the couple to roll across the room together and for the transition to happen once properly rather than faking it repeatedly. Any observers on the outside will immediately spot a successful attempt. The effect is of a body surfing a wave but it is not bodysurfing. Bodysurfing tends to rely on the 'surfer' being rigid and moving over several people rolling as 'waves'. This exercise can be done slowly with both participants relaxed. When it works, the transition of one body across the other is tender and magical.

Things to look out for include:

- *Participants not sticking to the simplicity of their task.* Encourage them to just roll, or just to try to connect and let it happen. Watch they don't throw themselves over their partner!
- *People gripping with their arms, making a literal hook around their partner.* As we have warned, this will make an effective connection but once they are moving, that arm will become trapped under their partner, they themselves will come crashing down on the other side as the roll completes, and they will then have their arm trapped under their partner as they begin to roll!
- *People being scared about giving their full weight.* This will happen and the result is often that they inadvertently concentrate their weight into smaller areas by lifting their head or rushing the move and trying to get off quickly. This results in them pressing their weight into their partners in a painful stiletto effect. Remind them that an equally distributed weight is easier to handle and that this exercise demands total relaxation and giving of this weight.
- *People just rushing through it without mastering the technique.* If they are doing it properly, they can do it at any speed.

Once this is working, have a play . . .

Place the rest of the group at the opposite end of the room and ask your volunteer couple to maintain eye contact with them as much as possible through the exercise. Try different types of music. Try different speeds. Ask them to assume the 'log' position with their eyes open, the 'rock' with their eyes closed. What theatrical contexts emerge? Is there a relationship between 'characters'? What if you gave them text? How does this challenge and reinvent the text? (And the movement?)

Rolling around on the floor with a partner is fun of course, but like the Rolling 1 exercise there is method in this. It is relevant to general contact work.

The person who is the 'log' is taking their partner's weight and slowly moving it. They are responsible for how that body gets moved and are in control. It might be useful to point out to them that they have done this without placing their hands on their partners. The momentum and strength has come from their core and not their extremities. Similarly, the 'rock' has made this possible by giving their partner their weight and not denying it. It was this that made the contact possible.

This is a fundamental lesson to learn.

Push Hands

This exercise was borrowed from Tai Chi and may be familiar to many in one form or another. Here it helps participants get used to the notion of non-verbal and essentially physical communication between performers.

Get the group into pairs. One partner puts their hand out, palm down, and the other partner places their hand on top of the other's hand. The person with the hand below pushes their hand upwards slightly so there is a gentle pressure between the two hands. The person with their hand on top is now in control. They can lead their partner around the room keeping their hand flat while their partner follows, trying to keep their hand flat and the pressure between the two constant. They can take their partner on a journey exploiting all levels without actually ending up on the floor (look out for people slipping their thumb around their partner's hand and thereby 'gripping'). To achieve this you have to relax your body and really concentrate on the signals your partner is sending through touch. As you may be asked to go all the way down to the floor, or walk quickly forward or backwards, you have to have your knees bent and be physically prepared to go anywhere.

It can be a group's mistake to interpret this exercise as an attempt to outwit your partner. It is important to stress that this exercise involves two people working together in an attempt to build a physical understanding. They should be working together to get better at it. With this in mind it helps to instruct the practitioners to be truthful and just stop and start again if they are losing the plot! Make sure they are being honest with each other about who is actually leading. Stopping is good and to be encouraged. It helps establish the limits and parameters and keeps the task simple.

Stop this exercise after a while. It may be that the room is experiencing varying degrees of success. Now instruct the person who is being led to close their eyes and concentrate fully on the touch of the hands only. Run the exercise again.

Debrief the group to find out if there was a greater success this time. Initially there may have been chaos until the followers could trust the leaders, but in our experience this exercise yields greater success when the eyes are closed and the focus is purely on the touch.

It should be pointed out that this touch and ability to communicate physically is the absolute bedrock to any contact work between partners. This simple exercise is applicable to all abilities and provides the perfect starting point or introduction to many more advanced exercises outlined later.

GAMES – A SELECTION OF CROWD PLEASERS

These games are used within Frantic Assembly workshops to animate and energise the room. Workshops can be intimidating to participants and we try to introduce the idea that this is going to be fun as well as challenging as soon as possible.

Some of the games have been picked up and adapted along the way. Others have been created to satisfy a need for energy, focus or training.

As with the constructive warm-up ideas, each one is used when we think they will complement or offer something instructive to the rest of the workshop.

Marcia Takedown

This incorporates an exercise introduced to us by Marcia Pook, a performer in our production *Underworld*. We think she originally picked it up from her time working for V-TOL Dance Company, but it may be one of those generic exercises that all dancers will recognise from their training. Here it is expanded to create a dynamic and exhausting exercise that quickly tests technique, builds trust and animates and energises the group.

Step 1

Split the group into pairs. One partner closes their eyes and trusts their partner from here on. The other partner places a flat hand gently on the back of their partner's neck and leads them around the space using the slightest pressure possible to indicate directions and speeds. Both partners are communicating through the area of contact, as in Push Hands.

Once the group are comfortable and showing signs of trusting each other, open the exercise out again. Allow anyone to take control of a random partner for a short time as they walk around the room before safely letting them go free again. Once this is working insist that the partner who is being guided closes their eyes the moment their partner takes control. They should think of this moment as liberating rather than frightening. They are not required to make any decisions but purely to concentrate on the minute fluctuations in touch from their partner's hand guiding them around the room. When the controlling partner wants to release them they give a small squeeze on the back of the neck and touch their shoulder. This is the sign to open their eyes and carry on walking normally, looking for people to take control of so that the relationship is constantly changing.

Try increasing the speed when the group appear to be working well. Instruct the group to cut down the duration of contact and make those moments more fleeting. This allows for many more moments of contact between different people. When they are almost at running speed you should notice how quickly people can turn from looking around the room for a victim to a completely trusting, passive partner with just the slightest touch on the back of the neck.

As with all exercises make sure this is advanced in very clear stages. If it is not and people start banging into each other, then any group trust will be lost. At this stage you could try the hand on different body parts. Aim to use more difficult connections, possibly not with hands. Try shoulders or hips.

Step 2

This next stage moves on from a trust exercise to a contact exercise. It is a very useful way to get the group thinking about how to work with people's weight, about using their own weight when moving people and not relying on strength.

The basic set-up of the previous stages still exists. The group walk around the space and anyone can place their hand on the neck of another. This time they only lead for a short time before giving their partner a squeeze on the neck (both partners keep their eyes open for this stage). This is the signal for the squeezed partner to gently take themselves to the floor and lie on their side.

From here they need to be rescued. The rules and technique of this engage- ment need to be clearly set out before this stage commences.

The person on the floor waits for someone to rescue them. To do this anyone can slide in behind them, spooning into them and placing their free/top arm around them, pulling themselves in as close to their partner as possible. This contact is crucial. Remind the practitioners that this contact is still the point of communication, as it was in Push Hands and in the stages above. The 'rescuer' pulls their partner towards them and rolls onto their other side, taking the partner with them. They keep this going and the partner rolls away once they reach the other side, then up onto their feet to resume walking. The rescuer keeps as fluid as possible and rolls away and gets up to carry on walking, awaiting the squeeze on the neck that will send them to the floor or looking out for people to rescue. Everyone in this game is a potential victim, everyone a potential rescuer. They have to work hard to keep the game alive with the emphasis being on rescuing.

The group may encounter some awkwardness in this exercise. People may be reluctant to give their weight, thinking they are crushing the person that they are rolling over. Similarly, if the rescuer does not concentrate on the contact between their stomach and the victim's back, then the move runs the risk of being an uncoordinated act of strength. If the victim senses this, then they are even more likely to withhold their weight. It needs to be pointed out to the victim that withholding or apologising for their weight can mean that they rush the move, throw themselves over the rescuer, or lift their head and legs up during the move. If they do this, they create a stiletto heel effect where their weight is given to the rescuer over a much smaller body area, thereby increasing the pressure on the rescuer. The only way to help the rescuer is to make as much contact as possible and move with the impetus they offer through the contact between back and front.

It is worth emphasising that we have thrown nothing away from the previous stages. We should not forget what we have learnt. We are just applying the same basic principles to more complex situations.

Step 3

This step is useful for all levels of ability. In Step 2 we can crank up the pace so that it becomes an intensive physical session. In Step 3 we have no choice. It is fast and furious.

Split the group up. If, for example, you have ten participants, split them up into two groups of five or groups of four and six (this will make it slightly easier; groups of five will be very hard work). The group of, say, four are now the victims. The group of six are the rescuers.

Take the group of six out of the space. Line them up and make them form a queue facing into the space. The group of four walk around the space and can randomly 'die', taking themselves to the floor and lying on their side. It is the task of the group of six, the 'rescuers', to storm into the space and rescue anyone dead on the floor as they did in Step 2. They are to spend as little time in the space as possible. The person at the front of the queue must do their duty and get out again to join the back of the queue, leaving a new person at the front of the line ready to go into action. As the victims choose to 'die' randomly it means that the rescuer at the front of the queue must be prepared to act quickly. Indeed the random nature means that it is possible for all the victims to 'die' at the same time, meaning that the first four rescuers in the line need to race in and save them and then race back to the queue. All through this it helps to shout, cheer, encourage, etc. from the sidelines. If you have a large group and therefore have spectators, have them roar at the 'savers' to react to the 'dying' and to get back out of the space as quickly as possible.

This can be an exhausting exercise. What we are looking for here is a commitment to the techniques already explored and mastered. If they start to panic, then it will all collapse. If they relax and don't think too much about it, then their contact can and usually does become much more fluid and dynamic. It is all a balancing act of technique, energy, adrenalin and confidence.

Step 4

Follow all this exertion up with a debrief session. It is very useful to ask whether people found it easier when they didn't have time to think about what they were doing or worry about being polite about where they are putting their hands! We often notice a marked improvement in the application of technique from this stage onwards. It should also be an opportunity to remind the participants of the simplicity of the route taken to this point, how they had to take little steps along the way. It is important to recognise these steps as time and time again that process of mastering bite-sized chunks will stand them in good stead.

Quad

This exercise is a Frantic favourite and is useful in getting people used to count structures. We are not sure where we picked it up. It is probably a generic theatre game, but we constantly adapt it to suit the groups we work with.

Firstly, the group should be placed in a grid formation or as close as possible to a grid in the event of having odd numbers. Everybody starts facing the same direction, which we shall call the 'front'. For the purposes of this book we shall imagine that there are 16 people, with 4 rows of 4.

Set a tempo by means of a music track or a simple count or rhythm and ask the front row to bounce on the spot eight times in unison. These should be small, light jumps with the shoulders and hands relaxed. The feet should be relaxed and we suggest that, when in the air, the feet should hang down towards the floor in a relaxed manner rather than tense and held with the toes pointing straight ahead. On the eighth count, the front row jump around through 180 degrees. We suggest that everyone turns in the same direction, e.g. clockwise. If all is correct, the front row should now be face to face with the second.

On the next 'one' count, the second row do the same thing, bouncing on the spot eight times, turning through 180 degrees on the eighth count. The third row pick up on the next count and repeat. When the count reaches the 'back' row, in this case the fourth row, they too take the next 'one' count and bounce on the spot eight times, turning clockwise through 180 degrees on the eighth count. As the back row they then continue, using the next 'one' count and bouncing on the spot, except that this time they turn back clockwise on the sixth count, at which point they are face to face with the third row. The third row copy and so on along to the front row who, after bouncing on the spot six times, will end up facing the 'front'. Using the next 'one' count, the first row then bounce for four counts before turning. This continues through the grid until it reaches the back row that then turns after just two counts. This moves through the grid to the front where the first row bounces twice before facing the front and immediately turning back on themselves after a count of just one. The other rows all follow.

Put simply, the group stand in grid formation and, using a simple bounce, turn after a count structure of 8, 6, 4, 2, and 1. This count structure could be adapted, e.g. 8, 7, 6, 5 or, for a more advanced group, something like 5, 3, 8, 3, 3, but we would suggest keeping it very simple to start with. Some of our most accomplished performers have fallen foul of what would seem to be the simple logic of this exercise. Even in using the basic count structure above, the group are still working with a complex rhythm, which is particularly apparent if using a music track in 4/4 time to accompany the exercise. At various points, the group will be counting 'across' the bars of the music, which always requires a little more focus.

Once the group seem to have the hang of the basic structure and counts, you might then introduce specific events on particular counts for the jumping group. One example might be to throw the right hand up into the air on the count of two. It is probably necessary to point out that this does not mean throwing the hand on every second count, only on the two itself. It is also important that this additional move should, like the feet, be relaxed; the hand should have weight in it and should feel like a hearty fling into the air before returning to the side, all within the single count.

Other events that might be thrown into the mix are a handclap, bringing the feet together while in mid-air on a given jump, or a shake of the head. You might even choose to bring in some vocal events. Putting the events on the same counts as the turns means that during the sequence, participants now have to manufacture a turn AND the prescribed event. This might influence the type of events you choose to add in.

An advanced version of this is an event for the standing groups. For example, on the count of 3, the 12 standing bodies are asked to sweep their right foot behind their left heel and then return to their standing position all within a single count. (Due to the visual nature of this event, we like to call it the 'Cat Litter Tray' move.)

In making the exercise more complicated, look out for shoulder tension in both the jumping and standing groups and also point out anyone clenching their fists. Often during this exercise you will witness the phenomenon of the body turning through a half turn and the head seeming to arrive a second later. This is not uncommon and we take it as a good signal that the body already has a rhythmic sense of the exercise and the head has yet to catch up.

(Note: We always suggest that all turns are made in the same direction, turning over either the left or the right shoulder. For some reason, the physical instinct seems to be to turn over one shoulder one way and then the other shoulder in order to return. In keeping it in the same shoulder, even the simple task of turning requires a little bit more thought and concentration.)

Quad Jump

Like many of these exercises, Quad Jump can start simple and be taken a lot further. It works best with a group of 8–12 people. You could always split larger groups into two and have one group watch as it is fun to observe.

Consider the four corners of the room. Place all of your group in the bottom right corner. Number them, e.g. 1–12. The first person sets off from the bottom right corner running towards the bottom left. They turn sharply and head towards the top left corner (they are running around the room clockwise). At this corner they have to create a manouvre that accomplishes a sharp 90 degree turn to the right. They then move on to the top right corner. Again they have to negotiate a turn of your choice. Having done so they then head back to the group in the bottom right corner.

Here the group have assembled themselves into a rough horseshoe shape to welcome the runner. As the runner runs into them they are lifted by the group high into the air, held for a second then returned to the ground and the second runner sets off on the same route.

The key to the group lift is the runner thinking about pressing their weight down into the hands while also thinking about going up. The lifters need to know where they are going to place their hands and absorb the energy of the inbound runner and transfer that horizontal energy into a vertical thrust that lifts the runner high above their heads. They should lock their arms at this point and ensure the weight is evenly distributed through the group.

The runner needs to know that they are aiming to make contact with one person at the back of the horseshoe. They plant their hands on that person's shoulders and press down. When they are up their hands should still be pressing down completely vertically, sending their weight down the body of this person. This person has their hands on the front of the runner's shoulders. (You can build towards versions where the runner just balances when they are up above the group and they do not press their hands down on the person at the back of the horseshoe. It is crucially important that the supporter has a good connection with the runner, however.)

The runner has to help with the lift. They do this not by jumping but by sending their weight forward rather than up. As they lean forward they should lift one leg behind them. This allows part of the group to get hold of it. As soon as the runner feels this leg lift off the floor they need to press down into it to allow the other leg to lift. They also need to imagine their backs being lifted or pulled up to make sure they do not sag during the lift.

Once they have been held for a second they need to be safely let back down again, feet first. The group need to negotiate their way through this.

The person at the back of the horseshoe should change for every runner and

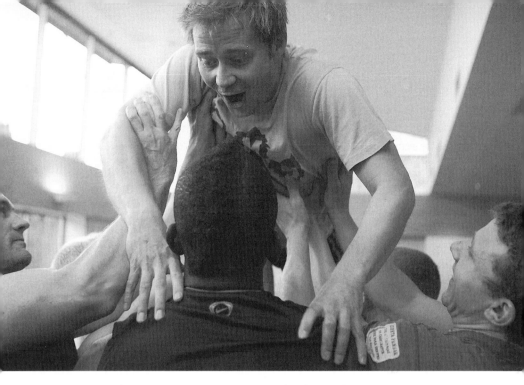

Eddie Kay being lifted by the cast during rehearsals for *Othello* © Manuel Harlan

they all need to keep alert to know which number runner is setting off and if they are next!

Start slow and steady, making sure everyone is confident and clear what is being asked of them. Warn against adrenalin taking over. Allow a couple of pedestrian rounds so that people can settle into it. As they do you can start to crank up the speed. Give them an exciting, pumping music track to help them. Things should improve quickly, but point out any tendency to jump or stall their momentum as they approach the lift-off moment.

There are a couple of ways to turn this into a more advanced exercise (and a much more exciting one too!).

Instead of waiting for the first runner to complete before the second runner sets off get the second runner to go when your first has reached the top left corner (the second base). This means that there are two runners at one time. This puts pressure on both runner and jumper to get it right and get it over with. The group must also organise themselves in such a way that someone who is crucial to the lift is not suddenly obliged to set off just as a runner is about to reach them! The group have to continually re-form and reorganise.

If your group are advanced and disciplined enough, you could turn the lift into a proper leap. The group still have to absorb the energy and translate it into a high lift. They have to be careful and adjust to the different forces exerted by different runners. The more confident and capable they are, the faster and further away the leap becomes. The dismount can be more choreographed too if you ask your group to find a route out of it that can serve the speed and precision of the whole Quad Jump task.

Clear the Space

This is a variation on what we are sure is a generic exercise that has been around for years. We include it here to show how we have morphed the exercise to fulfil the needs of a Frantic warm-up. This version has gone through many variations over the years and in some ways is at its best when used to respond to a space. The version here contains the most reliable elements we have found, but the simple nature of its form means that it is highly adaptable. We often use this exercise at the very start of a session in order to help participants get a sense of the room they are working in. It is also useful in breaking down physical inhibitions as the instructions come fairly rapidly, giving people no time to worry about contact with other bodies in the space!

We advise describing all of the instructions *before* starting this exercise in order to allow it to flow once begun.

Start the group off by asking them to simply walk around the space for a minute or so. Ask them to imagine that regular pedestrian speed is 100% and, for the sake of this exercise, all walking is at 105%. Even the simple task of walking has a little bit more energy involved, a little more intention. This helps to charge the room and raise physical awareness among the group as they negotiate their bodies in space. They should be asked to consider just what it means for this number of people to be moving in this particular space and at this particular speed. Once the group seem comfortable with this, start to throw in any number of the instructions listed below. At first, the rate of incidence should be kept fairly low, not least of all for the sake of safety, particularly if the room is quite small. Once the group show signs of confidence, increase the rate of the instructions to the point where sometimes one instruction might not yet be complete before the next one is given. Allow each instruction to occur a couple of times before adding in another one. All instructions should be carried out as *quickly* as possible. Once each instruction is complete, say 'go' to signify a return to walking (which should be maintained at 105% speed).

Clear the space: The whole group must move to the outsides of the room and place both hands on a wall surface. It might be necessary to limit this instruction to certain sides of the room, for instance if one wall is all windows which might be open on a hot day!

Centre: Having established a centre point in the room for the group, they have to stand as close to one another as possible in the centre spot. Once in place, the group rest their head on whoever and whatever is nearest. It is important to point out the two-part nature of this instruction. The group need to come together as closely as possible *before* resting their head. The reverse might lead to some serious floor cleaning issues. Check that the group are responding to a single 'centre' of the room. The collective huddle should not look like a string of people but one single 'blob', with no satellite groups hanging off.

Fold: Participants take themselves down to the floor in a fluid spiral motion and pull themselves into the foetal position, resting their head on the floor. For this, the group must make good use of the room and be aware of the proximity of each other. In simple terms, they should get themselves to the floor as quickly and efficiently as possible, taking care to avoid impacting the elbows and knees on the way down. Use the instruction 'Unfold' to get the group to reverse this and get them back to a standing position. In unfolding, participants should use the same idea of a spiralling motion that takes them from the floor to standing.

Look: Everyone stands completely still and looks directly into the eyes of any other member of the group. It does not matter if the gaze is not met. They should remain fixed in this way until another instruction is given.

Favourite: Ask each participant to choose a favourite part of the room. This should not be another person and needs to remain a constant. On hearing the instruction 'Favourite' they must come to a complete standstill and, using their right arm and first finger, point and look directly at their own favourite part of the room. Push for the response time on this particular instruction to be as sharp and fast as possible.

Person: On this instruction, each participant grabs the nearest person and pulls them into a hug. They should only embrace in pairs here, not least of all to provide an incentive not to be the one person who remains hug-less if the group are an odd number. In hugging their partner, each person should be seen to be pulling their partner's back in towards their own front and effectively squeezing the air out of the space between them. There should be no chance of seeing daylight between their bodies at all. They should also keep squeezing throughout, sensitising their fingertips, which should be pressed into the back of their partner. Don't let people off here. Make sure they commit fully to the hug. If you make sure they do the first one properly then, when the game speeds up, they will be doing it properly without thinking about it.

Stereo/Teacher: This instruction should make specific use of an element in the room – the LED display on stereo equipment or the eyes of a teacher who may be sat at the side of the room for instance. On hearing the appropriate instruction (we'll use 'Stereo' for this example), the entire group should run towards the element and sit together cross-legged as close as possible with all their eyes focused on the stereo. Like 'Fold', this instruction needs the group to pay particular attention to one another and the space provided by the room.

Once the group have a solid understanding of the different instructions and have a good, quick response time to each one, it is then possible to be creative with the order in which the instructions are given. One example is to give the instruction 'Fold' and then, once the group are in full contact with the floor, give the instruction 'Favourite'. In order to achieve the instruction with maximum economy they should not return to standing but shift from the foetal position and twist themselves into a position that allows them to see and point out their favourite part of the room. This added task of economy in following one instruction after another might also be exercised by following the instruction 'Stereo' with either 'Favourite' or 'Person' – a combination of all three in various orders is always a good finishing point.

Advanced versions of this game might involve the instruction 'Different Side Clear', which should only follow a 'Clear' command, at which point the entire group need to choose another wall to make contact with. This instruction sees the entire group pass through the space and requires some spatial negotiation. 'Different Person' works in much the same way, following a 'Person' command. To advance this instruction even further, there is the instruction after 'Different Person' to then return and find the person you were hugging just prior to the instruction. We have yet to give this instruction a permanent title. Any thoughts here are welcome via our website (www.franticassembly.co.uk/p127.html).

This game should be both energetic and precise. Instructions such as 'Person' should be closely monitored to ensure that the group are committing to full body contact. The 'Person' instruction also works best if the group are an odd number. By stressing that the instruction means that people are only allowed to pair up, there should always be one person left out. Asking the group to make sure that they do not become the one left out is a good impetus for creating a room full of people desperate to grab hold of a body, any body! By stressing that nobody ought to be the one left out more than once, you only heighten this effect.

Relays

We often include relays in our warm-ups with large groups. These can be simple shuttle runs to a point and back, handing over to the next person to do the same, or they can be more complicated.

The relays are very useful. Often when we are working with a large group for the first time, they can be nervous, apprehensive about what they are going to be doing. They might think that the session is going to be serious and exhausting. They might have all kinds of preconceptions about us, theatre, or physical theatre. The relays quickly introduce an element of fun. Once participants realise that fun is allowed they are generally much more relaxed.

The first relay

We always start with the simplest version. We split the group into teams. Getting them all to stand in a line and then going along the line numbering them 1, 2, 3, 4, 1, 2, 3, 4, etc. will provide four teams of number 1s, 2s, 3s and 4s. This also splits friends and same-sex groups up.

Place the groups at one end of the room and place an object (a book, a trainer, etc.) opposite each group at the other side of the room, leaving plenty of space from the wall.

Tell them this is a race, but most importantly lay out a couple of clear ground rules:

1   You must touch the object.
2   When you return you must touch RIGHT hands with the next person. This means that the person running back will always pass on the right side of the person setting off. It means there is little chance of confusion and collision when the adrenalin is pumping and everyone is desperate to win.
3   You should make as much noise as possible when cheering your team on.

Create a bit of tension before the 'go' moment. It should feel like pure play but there are important things happening here. The group are focused and are about to be energised. They are listening to you avidly and are following clear instructions to the letter. They are about to start thinking like a team. They are about to feel as though getting something right matters.

The second relay

Things are getting more complicated and more physically risky here. By now they are usually hooked and energised and really want to know how this relay will differ from the first. They will also want to make amends for a loss in the first round or keep up their winning record.

It is best to demonstrate this exercise. Walk it through with a group of volunteers.

1   The first runner sets off and touches the object at the other end of the room. They run back and offer their hand to the next person.
2   They hold hands and set off towards the object but the first person is now running backwards, leading the second. The second person must instruct the first (who is running backwards) that they are approaching the object. When they get to the object they must both touch it. This is what releases the second runner to head back to pick up the third. (The first stays down the other end of the room with the object.)
3   The second runner connects with the third and then runs backwards, leading the third across the room. As runner 2 heads backwards as quickly as possible without losing contact with their partner, the first runner, now waiting at the other end of the room, waits to safely guide the second runner 'home'. Anyone left by the object has to remain active and safely guide the backwards runner home.
4   The relay ends when the last person has been led to the object and the whole group run together back to the side they started on.

Again they need to encourage each other and create some noise but they also need to remain active and aware. They are all working as a team, pushing each other along but also making sure everyone is safe.

This relay is such a simple way to get a group working as a team without them having to think about it.

The third relay

If you ever need to break the ice, this exercise is great at addressing that reserve in a new group.

Make sure that the object you placed at the end of the room has plenty of space around it.

1   The first runner sets off down the room and runs *around* the object.
2   They head back and when they reach the next person, the first runner turns around, puts their right arm through their own legs and reaches for the left hand of the next runner.
3   They set off down the room as fast as they can, the first runner hunched over but leading the second.
4   They run around the object.
5   When they head back they need to turn around so that the second runner can put their right hand between their legs and reach for the left hand of the third runner.
6   The three of them set off again. Continue.

The group gets longer and more absurd. They are not allowed to break the chain. If they do, they must stop, link up and continue again. They also need to find a speed that suits the whole group – the first runner cannot just run around corners at their own pace as centrifugal force would send the people at the back through the walls.

The relay ends with the whole group going around the object and making it back to their starting place.

Another relay

If your room and floor surface will allow this, try another relay (it adapts the first relay but should be used in addition and should not replace it).

For this you need to make sure the group can all slide on the floor on their thighs. They need to put a hand down onto the floor and push their hips forward, sliding on their hip/thigh while pushing away from the hand they put on the floor. They need to make good contact with the floor and avoid dropping onto knees or shuffling on feet. You should be looking for a smooth downward curve towards the floor rather than a crunch of bone and dancefloor.

If this is in place, the relay then basically involves participants running towards the wall and sliding to the floor as they arrive there, using their feet to soften into the wall and push off in the opposite direction. It should give them the propulsion a swimmer looks for in their tumble turn. Apart from this it is the same as the first relay.

Relay slalom

This relay is advanced only insofar as it requires people to have a good, solid grasp of spatial awareness in order to eliminate risk.

The initial set-up follows that of the first relay with the teams numbered in one corner of the room and an object some distance from the wall in the opposite corner. By number each individual runs at a regular speed across the room, around the far object and returns to tag the right hand of the next runner as specified earlier. It might be necessary to point out the importance of efficient cornering around the end object, leaning into and over the object rather than out and away, to increase efficiency and time.

From here, a second object is placed to the far left of the room, about a third of the way along the route, and a further object to the far right, two-thirds of the way down. This time, each person should set off from the corner and run over to the far left object, passing along the outside. They then move across the space to pass along the right-hand side of the object placed two-thirds down the room on the right. To complete the slalom they then run towards the original object in the opposite corner, passing along the left-hand side of the object and around it before running straight up through the middle of the room to tag the next person.

An advanced version of this sees participants running down through the space at a regular speed and then returning up through the middle at a sprinting speed, i.e. as fast as possible.

A further version (and the one that calls on good powers of spatial awareness) is where, after the first person has set off and passed the second of the three objects down the slalom trail, number two sets off. Runner 3 sets off as runner 2 passes the second object and so on. This creates a sweeping field of running subjects, some moving at regular running speed and others at full sprint. It is a great exercise in testing the response time of a group operating at speed. Further versions might involve more slalom objects along the length of the diagonal or people setting off at even shorter intervals one after another for a really invigorating field of runners.

Eye contact

Eye contact is such an important part of performance and theatre. When it happens you know you are being spoken to directly. There is no confusion and that recognition is instant. Yet it can be one of the more terrifying tasks for young practitioners and students to master.

The inexperienced may think that being on stage puts the performer in a position of vulnerability or weakness because there are 300 pairs of eyes watching them. But that is a position of strength. Like holding a stick out in front of a dog, you can capture an audience's gaze and guide it left or right with the flick of a wrist. Magicians know only too well how easy it is to pretend to throw the stick for the audience, sending us all looking in the wrong direction. That is a position of strength.

If you were to confront those 300 pairs of eyes one pair at a time, then you would very quickly understand where the strength lies. Watch the intimidating crowd become full of intimidated individuals! This is not to say that we are looking for a confrontational and aggressive form of theatre, although it does the more nervous performer no harm to experience this power for a while. Eye contact is also a way towards a warmer and more inclusive form of theatre.

The following are games we use to highlight the power and immediacy of eye contact.

Eye Bounce

Put your group in pairs. Get them to spread around the room but stand opposite each other. In this exercise they need to bounce opposite their partner.

One of them is to start bouncing high into the air. The other watches and takes on the timing of their partner. What they have to do now is bounce up as their partner is coming down. They should try to maintain this piston action and keep looking ahead.

The couple will start to lose that rhythm and will begin to jump at the same time. Before this they will make eye contact. It will be sudden but irrefutable. Even though they are trying to concentrate on something else they will instantly become aware of the moment they make eye contact.

Eye Stealing

In this exercise we visualise the contact between the eyes as something physical. Participants work in pairs again and stand facing one another. They are asked to imagine a sticky web stretching from a point between the eyes of one of them to the same point on the participant they are making eye contact with.

Name one of the couple A and the other B.

A leads B around the room. They do not make physical contact. It is up to B to maintain the distance between both partners (about 60 cm).

This means that participants have to be centred, responsive, and relaxed. It is not A's job to ask the impossible. Just like Push Hands this should be two people trying to get better at something and not A trying to make a fool out of B.

The couple will move around the room with a fixed distance between them. Eventually they can take this a bit further and move it onto the floor. This might involve contact but initially look out for couples over-elaborating. It might help to create a rule of 'no going to the floor' when you first start.

Use a couple to demonstrate the next stage. Add a third person, C, into the equation. C will move with A and B but will be looking for opportunities to 'steal' the gaze of one of them. They do this by manoeuvring themselves into the gap between A and B and allowing their eyes to make contact with one of the partners. Just like Eye Bounce, the moment of eye contact is unequivocal.

When they make contact C then takes control and will lead the partner they have just stolen around the room with the same fixed distance (60 cm) between them. The person now not involved becomes the next 'stealer' and must look for opportunities to intercept a couple.

Regardless of whether you are a leader (A) or a follower (B), if the 'stealer' makes eye contact with you, you must immediately follow them.

These are both fun games to build up confidence and performance strength. We feel that basics, like eye contact, should not be taken for granted. Playing with eye contact can be very empowering for the participant.

Jump Tag

Like the relays, this exercise starts with a concept any group would understand and then takes it further.

The game is basically like 'Stuck in the Mud' where the person who is 'on' tries to tag those running away from them. When they are tagged participants would normally stand still with their legs open and wait for rescuers to slide through and free them. They are both then free to escape from the person who is 'on'.

In our version the people who are tagged stand prepared to receive a rescuer who will run and jump into their arms. The tagged person will hold them in a cradle lift and then return them to the floor, feet first, ready to escape again. This can become very dynamic but should start safe and pedestrian. If this is not an experienced group, then you should take them through a safe jumping, lifting and holding technique.

Make sure the jumper is aiming to have the core of their body arrive at their partner's chest height. They should be hitting their partner at the top of the parabola of the jump and not be dropping down into their arms. That way lies injury!

Make sure the catcher is breathing out when they catch.

Instruct them both to pull in towards each other once the leap/catch is complete. This squeeze is held securely for a second before the jumper is gently and smoothly returned to the floor (see 'Ways into basic lifting techniques', page 148).

They should also be instructed on how to return their partner to the ground safely. It is also very important to remind people that being lifted is actually a very active role. To illustrate this you could instruct two able people to perform a cradle lift. From the outside this will look like the lifter is active and the lifted is passive. This is our romantic preconception.

Now instruct the lifted person to squeeze themselves into the lifter and have their arms around the lifter's neck pressing down on their shoulders as much as they can. Instruct the lifter to gradually take their arms away. The lifted person has to work hard at keeping themselves close to the lifter, engaging their stomach muscles throughout.

It is, of course, up to you to gauge whether your group can safely take on this game. An experienced group can really push the dynamism of this exercise.

They can increase the speed and distance of the leap into the arms, and the return to the ground can also become more dynamic. Really experienced groups can even freestyle on the jump, testing the catcher's reactions and technique. (You can build up to this, replacing the leap and catch with a lift.)

Despite the meticulous preparation and training that goes into this exercise, it is ultimately about a group of energised participants testing and responding to each other instinctively. These results don't come instantly but they are well worth aiming for.

chapter five

Choreography

What we mean by 'choreography'

By choreography we mean any formalised movements that become set and can be repeated. This can be the dynamic and spectacular or it could be the minute and precise. It can be explosive and it can be introspective. We will not go into notation here (we film everything anyway) as what is important is the process behind the genesis of the choreography, not the choreography itself.

When we have visited schools, colleges and universities, or even when we have been talking to fledgling devising companies, the same question about creating choreography comes up. How do you get started? After further discussion we have usually found that people are over-complicating their attempts to make choreography. They are often bogged down in attaching meaning to moves. This can make the creative process unbearably heavy. If you approach making choreography this way, you might find the process impossible.

This chapter aims to demystify the creative process. Each exercise tries to be as simple as possible and you will notice that meaning is hardly ever addressed. If it is, it is always at the end of the process and emerges through directorial manipulation. Our hope is that, as meaning is separated from process, you can take the process on to create choreography for new and different contexts.

Neil Bettles and Cait Davis from the film *Hide and Seek*, 2006 (see Web site)

Stopping Points and Connections

This building exercise was employed in the early days of the tenth anniversary revival of *Hymns*. It can be easily translated for your own needs.

The four performers were asked to pair up in the space. They were asked to move around a most basic set of randomly placed chairs. They could sit or stand or move in any way but they had to take the impulse for their starting points and finishing points from their partner's movements. What you have is performers listening closely to each other, using their peripheral vision to key into the quality and timing of their partner's moves. At no time do they mimic or mirror the actual physical movements of another performer. It is only the quality and timing of the moves that connect the partners. Both sets of partners share the space but never become aware of the other pair. What appears is a scene of four individuals whose physicality or body language is subconsciously connected. As one person moves, another might connect with them and move as if being pushed or pulled across the space. They do not touch but there appears to be a clear connection across the space between them. The small movement of a person's arm may appear to be connected to the completely different move of another person. It is important that they don't do identical moves but just try to discover moves that have a similar quality and dynamic. Very quickly little stories and connections appear and disappear like fireworks. It is very important to note this effect as already you may have found a key to telling complex stories through physical suggestion and not words.

This was a crucial stage in the development of the performers. They needed to get a sense of the potential economy of physical storytelling. By storytelling we mean the visual presentation of a complex emotional situation through simple physicality. The story at this stage is very much in the eye of the beholder and is an early example of how important the role of the audience is when we make our work.

As a result of this the performer learns to avoid the temptation to 'tell' the story with their moves, to only do sad or frustrated moves to show sadness and frustration. It is only your audience at this stage who are reading any story; the performers are simply committing to a physical task and are not trying to tell a story. Even when we get to that stage, we might find out that the character's understanding of the context may be completely different from that of the audience. It is a reminder that 'theatre' may well be what happens when performance meets the audience. Does it really exist without their consideration? Remember that the sadness of a scene may truly lie in the audience's reaction, in their judging it to be a sad situation. For example, a character who feels there is no hope when the audience knows there is none is sad. A character who feels hope when the audience knows there is none is utterly tragic.

We wanted to move on very quickly from here but we identified that if the performers were not to capture this quality of communication, then we would never be able to work at the rate we felt we needed to. As it turned out, the exercise can be made much more complex before the need to move on. This simple exercise may suggest a situation where the physicality of four performers would scream a whole spectrum of desires, needs, grievances without ever saying a word. As this was only an exercise and did not directly become a scene, it served to instruct the performers of the importance of body language in our work. It quickly unearthed an incredibly rich subtext.

It is very important not to think that we like to throw out deliberately obscure work towards our audience on the understanding that they will make something of it and that 'everyone will have a different interpretation anyway'. This might be a valid approach for some practitioners, but it is not a theory that we sign up to. Through our use of physicality and movement we found we are always inviting and guiding the audience towards our preferred conclusion. We don't have to spell it out for them in every action. We realised that it was so important to engage the audience and not just present what we feel they need to understand. This can feel like being battered around the head for an audience. We always try to imagine what will bring our audience forward in their chairs, what will send them reeling backwards. What is it that animates and activates our audience? In fine art terms, we are Impressionists rather than Surrealists. The Impressionist uses a variety of colours and textures to elicit an almost emotional response from the viewer but always guides the viewer towards an understanding of what is being presented, e.g. through the title.

> Try to make Monsieur Pissarro understand that trees are not violet; that the sky is not the colour of fresh butter . . . and that no human being could countenance such aberrations . . . Try to explain to Monsieur Renoir that a woman's torso is not a mass of decomposing flesh with those purplish-green stains.
>
> (Albert Wolff, art critic, *Vigztoon* 1876)

It was at this stage that we started to harness the potential of the exercise and move towards its possible use in performance. The exercise was carefully moved closer to the theatrical context of *Hymns*; of four men contemplating the loss of a friend and desperately wanting to say the right thing. The stillness of the physicality was now informed by the context; the subtext remained rich

Steven Hoggett in *Hymns*, 2005

and full of possibilities; the performers were now clearly characters, complex in their silence. We found with this exercise that what the characters don't say is what they need to say and that the audience plays a crucial role in articulating the unsaid.

It was vital not to rush this transition from what can be considered 'play' into 'work'. It is worth noting that the temptation when working on your first section of a production is to 'solve' it rather than open out possibilities. The subtle blending of 'play' and 'work' liberates the performer from this expectation and allows them to explore freely while the director/outside eye helps collate and store all of this new information.

This exercise was very useful for the performance style that dominated *Hymns* but it serves as a much more general exercise too. Sometimes our attempts at naturalism can smother the more subtle body language. This exercise creates a dance out of that unconscious body language, revealing what we are screaming from the inside, and it is really important for us not to bury that physicality under extraneous movement. It serves to remind the performers that they are responsible for every move they make, that every move they make has a reaction or impact upon someone else, that a well-trained audience eye is looking keenly for the story beneath the surface. Within *Hymns* it meant that every moment on stage was considered. Moments are held. Physicality is awkward. It gives the impression of people physically and emotionally holding back.

'Listening' to each other physically

At every stage of working together we ask performers and students to listen to each other physically. We call it 'listening' but it is actually the use of peripheral vision, sensitivity to touch and just learning to communicate non-verbally with your fellow performers. This is the building block for all our physical work.

Round/By/Through

This exercise asks participants to create a string of material that has them moving all about and through their partner. It is simple and requires fluidity and balance. The words 'Round', 'By' and 'Through' are there to assist this process in that they offer a physical vocabulary to get started with and can be referred to if the couple (or three) become stuck or begin to over-complicate things.

This is one of a series of exercises that are useful in the initial stages of developing movement skills and material. As such, it should be considered in terms of providing a series of building blocks, both as a principle and as a practice. As a group of exercises they share a common principle, which is that, for the most part, they should be attempted as neutrally as possible. This means that they should only be infused with emotional meaning or character or relevant performance instinct towards the end. In this way, we keep the exercise open to possibilities. With exercises like this it is also useful to keep the end point out of sight and hopefully prevent performers falling into known patterns of physical behaviour. (By this we mean dance practices just as much as physical character practices – individuals should be equally discouraged from imbuing this exercise with flashes of contemporary dance styles as much as anybody demonstrating their 'person in lust' physicality.) The exercise works best in pairs but is also possible for groups of three. With this exercise it is entirely possible to have the start of a fairly complex looking duet up and on its feet within 20 minutes.

The partners stand opposite one another and choose A and B status. A is then given the task of changing the physical and spatial configuration between the two using any one of the instructions 'Round,' 'By' or 'Through'.

The term 'Round' here is chosen to represent any move that involves passing closely around the body of the partner. From this initial position, using around as the principle for movement, A might move around B to a point where they are now back to back or where A's front is pressed into B's back or A is standing with their front pressed in at 90 degrees to B's shoulder. 'Round' will normally involve some form of rotation in the hips of the person moving and normally some degree of circular movement around the partner, however small.

'By' is a term that comes into effect as a consequence of the actions 'Round' and 'Through' where either one of these two actions has created a space between the two partners. 'By' is the means by which the space that exists between the two is constantly reduced to as small a space as possible. Partners are encouraged to squeeze the air out from between their bodies during this exercise, to work in close proximity. This proximity should be considered at all times and should never be so close that it inhibits natural or free movement. 'By' should feel like a 'slotting in' move that is neat and efficient, a linking device to produce flow and possibility between the moves being created.

'Through' is the idea of passing through the partner and for the most part should be confined to the use of the upper body and arms. (More advanced groups might try using the lower body and be particularly vigilant in avoiding stock physicality.) A simple example of 'Through' would be for A to start off by using first their fingertips to make contact with the inner elbow of B and create space between B's ribcage and arm. This creation of space should be as economical as possible, with just enough room being made for A to pass their body through. For their part, B should neither help nor hinder this moment. A should be able to feel the full weight of B's arm in attempting this part of the exercise. The variety to be found here lies in the various ways in which A might pass through the space created by B's body – whether the fingers and hand continue to be the first body parts to pass through this newly made space or whether it is another body part such as the back of the right hip that passes through, creating a sense of A's body 'reversing' into the allocated space. Other points to pass through first might be the shoulders or the back of the neck. Rolling the outer hip in towards the partner when passing through is a very different dynamic from when the body rolls the same hip out and away from the partner. With confidence, it might be that the creation of the space on B's body is not initiated by the fingertips but by the elbow or the shoulder or forearm. Again, it is important that the partner gives full weight to the body part being acted upon. In the event of A moving 'Through', B should also be seen to close down the space created by A as soon as possible, i.e. as soon as that space is no longer needed or useful.

As a structure, we would usually ask the pairs to create a string of material involving between 12 and 16 moments, with the responsibility for movement switching between the two partners. In the instance of A having created the first three moments, B would then start from the configuration point that the pair find themselves in at the end of those first three moments. In this sense, the exercise is a cumulative one. Be on the look-out for 'shifts', which is where, at the end of A's sequence, one or both of the pair shift themselves, some-times very slightly, into a position that feels more comfortable as a starting point. It is important to point out that this is unnecessary and to encourage the participants to use whatever they are given as their starting point.

Once the string has been created, an important next step is to consider the entire sequence as one arc of events. Usually, due to the way in which this material has been created, when running the string there will be pauses (some-times very small, sometimes not) at the points where the responsibility for movement switches from one partner to another. These moments halt the flow of the string and it takes particular focus and attention to remove these pauses and create a string that has a beginning and an end rather than three or four observable 'chunks'. This part of the exercise is important in under-standing the flow involved in the transfer of energy and responsibility in both a visual and a physical sense.

Throughout this part of the exercise, it is important to remind the pairs not to imbue the material with intention at this stage. It is very easy, even at the first stages of this exercise, for the material to seem either 'fighty' (hands heavy, bodies seemingly flung into configurations suggesting aggression) or 'dancy' (hands floating delicately around the partner without making real contact or involving any true weight). Both of these types of event should be avoided.

The next step is to play with intention. One way for us came out of rehearsals for *pool (no water)*. During a development period, Mark Ravenhill observed us creating 'Round/By/Through' strings and then, in pairs, gave us slips of paper showing different ways in which to present the material. These pieces of paper contained words such as 'educate', 'protect', 'forget', 'insist', inspire', 'amuse', 'regret', etc. Adding this element is a great tool for starting to understand the communicative nature of movement. The observing participants were asked to guess what the informing word was and in most cases the group were correct or close without the rendition being ridiculously overt. It also asks the

Leah Muller, *pool (no water)*, 2006

performers to bring into play their interpretative skills when performing movement – a delicate first step along the essential path of creating movement that has meaning.

The eventual scene we created never made it into the final version of *pool (no water)* but involved one of the performers (A) being acted upon by not one but three others (B's) who were all 'Round/By/Through'-ing at the same time, examining the 'patient' with inquisitive detail that became more and more intrusive. For this version, the patient remained pedestrian throughout. This development created some fascinating physical opportunities between the three B's, who often used the end of another B's interactive moment as the start of their own. This exercise requires an A that is physically very responsive and doesn't mind being pulled around the room for a couple of hours in a way that is far from hospitable.

Round/By/Through is one of the most important building blocks we use when creating contact work. It can be the first solid step towards much more complex choreography.

Sign Describe

We developed this exercise through working with Graeae Theatre Company, who are notable for their work with disabled actors. We collaborated with them on the production *On Blindness*, which featured a cast of six performers. Among the company there was one blind actor and one deaf actor. As part of the rehearsal process we were all given extensive training in British Sign Language (BSL) as a means of communicating with one another. For a company obsessed with physical means of communication it was an intense and invigorating period. For a start there was the practical procedure of there only being one person able to speak in the room at any one time so as to allow the interpreters to be able to fulfil their role effectively. It is only in circumstances like this that we come to understand the nature of a Frantic rehearsal room, which often involves multi-narrative events all over the room. At times this new mode of operation felt like a restriction and on other days it felt like the most focused process we had ever enjoyed.

As part of creating a way in which we might all communicate effectively, Jenny Sealey, Artistic Director with Graeae, ran an exercise on day one, which involved us creating a sign name for ourselves, which would then be used by the rest of the company. Jenny explained that it should conform to the standards of BSL, which meant that the sign name should involve the hands, and operate in a TV-sized space in front of the chest and stomach area. We were encouraged to 'make up' our own sign language, the focus of the exercise being to create a physical gesture that matched the individual. This gesture could be representative of a physical characteristic or gestural trait, a physical habit or even the way we felt that particular morning (more on this later). This creative licence became pivotal in us creating a system that allowed us all to connect over the rehearsals and beyond, into the performance itself and then further into our social modes of communication while touring. (There was something very refreshing about being part of a full company that were able to sign effectively with each other in even the noisiest of environments – our voices during that tour were on spectacularly fine form if our memory serves . . .)

The following was developed from this period and is a great exercise in asking participants to physically 'get stuck in' to one another. In this way it is often used by us when encountering a new group for the first time – setting a strict task that forces the individual to explore another body in some detail. As with any exercise of this kind, observing the group is important and more often than not we impose quite a short time period within which the task must be achieved.

Split the group into pairs, with each pair assigning themselves an A and B status. For the next few minutes, A is to remain standing and should neither resist nor help B in their task. They should stand with their feet hip width apart in a comfortable stance with their hands relaxed at their sides and their eyes open throughout.

B has the task of discovering something about A that A probably doesn't know about themselves. In order to achieve this they are to examine the body using three categories.

Visual evidence

Using the eyes, B scans A's entire visible body, paying particular attention to the parts of A's body that A has probably never seen, e.g. back of the neck, behind the ears, behind the upper arm. They should also take in every part of skin that is visible, looking for distinct markings, blemishes, birthmarks, colourings and shadings. The visual examination should be thorough, checking minute detail such as eyes, hairline, earlobes, cuticles, inner elbows, etc.

Frame

B examines the body using their hands, paying particular attention to the frame of A. This might be shoulders, elbows, knees, ankles, hips – in short, any part of the skeleton – to check for any idiosyncratic details such as knobbles, bumps, lumps and smoothness.

Measurements

B takes measurements of A's body but not in any metric or imperial sense. Instead they measure A in relation to themselves. This might be with identical body parts, creating a direct comparison, e.g. whether A has a larger hand span than B. Alternatively, and perhaps more interesting, this might involve different body parts, e.g. measuring the width of the back of A in relation to B's hand span or the distance between A's eyebrows in relation to the digits of B's index finger.

We normally find it useful to place a time limit on this task, usually between two and three minutes, during which time B has to discover as many 'facts' about A as possible using all three methods of examination in the time allotted. At no point do they give any signal to A as to what it is they have discovered.

At the end of the two or three minutes (usually a music track), the roles are reversed and A now attempts to make discoveries about B. By making the time short, participants are pressed into action and should consider the body of their partner as an object that has to yield as many secrets as possible in a very short space of time.

Once this stage has been completed, each participant is asked to choose just one of the 'facts' that they have discovered about their partner. In having several to choose from, A's and B's should be encouraged to choose the detail that the partner is unlikely to know about themselves. From this 'fact' each then needs to create a simple grammatical sentence in their heads that relays this fact, e.g. 'A's back is the same width as three of my [B's] hand spans'. Once this sentence is clear in the mind, everyone should then create a gestural string to represent this sentence.

The gestural string should operate in the same way as BSL – that is, using the hands as a means of communicating and spatially working within the TV-sized space in front of the chest area. Note that, like BSL, the string need only communicate the essential details. Given a sentence like 'A's back is the same width as three of my hand spans', the words 'is', 'the', 'as' and 'of' would not be translated. In this way, the string is truly economical in the information that it seeks to convey. In our case, in the absence of knowing what the exact sign language was, Jenny Sealey always encouraged us to be inventive and attempt what we might imagine the sign to be for any word that challenged us, on the understanding that this in itself would, more often than not, convey meaning, even if not entirely accurately. With this exercise, it is important to encourage inventiveness. It is not an exercise in seeing how close we might be to actual BSL or any other form of signing. Again, we often place a time limit on this part of the exercise of two to three minutes. This should be an instinctive, reflective part of the exercise using physical intuition. We usually suggest that it is important only that the string makes true sense to the individual.

The basic version of this exercise culminates in the group then demonstrating their findings to one another. This can be done in a variety of ways. We normally form a circle with the pairs standing beside one another. They start by individually running through their gestural string, communicating the physical information to the rest of the group. They then tell the group verbally what it is they found, speaking aloud the sentence they constructed upon which the gestural string was based.

The advanced version is a first step in tackling the difficult challenge of combining text and movement. A runs through the gestural sequence alone, communicating the physical information to the entire group. They then repeat the gestural string, except this time they also speak the sentence at the same time. Both the gestural string and the spoken sentence should run alongside one another, starting and finishing at the same time.

The very simple task of effectively combining text and movement is often the undoing of many a budding physical theatre performer. By 'effective' it is probably important for us to define what it is we wish to avoid. In many circumstances (and, unfortunately, in many public performances) the collision between text and movement results in a scenario where the movement does have quite an agreeable and logical flow, but as a consequence, the rhythm of the sentence somehow becomes tied to that of the movement, producing what we call 'physical theatre speak'. This is when the natural rhythms of any given sentence are suddenly lost and instead the line or lines adopt a broken, irregular sound with odd stresses, falterings and hesitancies. Of course this is the only possible outcome when the rhythm of the sentence is being dictated by that of the movement. For us, this 'making strange' of language is highly undesirable. The natural rhythms and cadences of language are what we aspire to so that the spoken and physical languages truly coexist in tandem alongside one another in what one might call harmony.

This is not a simple task at all and as a company we have spent years and years wrestling with this challenge. Even a simple sentence like 'A's back is the same width as three of my hand spans' can come undone quite spectacularly when run alongside what is also a simple gestural sentence. For the above exercise, we ask that the verbal and gestural run alongside one another, each unaffected by the other in terms of rhythm, with nothing 'made strange'.

Sign Describe is a great exercise for bypassing the common fears of physical contact among a group. The task should be brisk, lively and light. Music tracks used here should also embody these qualities. Pushing the task element can often be the key to the success of this exercise. What often results are fantastic, detailed insights into one another, new information revealed and startling personal discoveries. Pleasure is often found not only in the observations made but also in the gestural ways in which people choose to represent their findings.

Sign Name Circle

An offshoot of this exercise has been our adaptation of an old, well-worn theatre game. Name Circle has probably had a variety of different names for the numerous groups that have used it over the years. In it, the company stand in a circle facing inwards. One member makes eye contact with another member of the group and begins to walk across the circle in a straight line towards them, maintaining eye contact. The person on the receiving end of this has to name the person striding towards them. The receiver then establishes eye contact with a different person in the circle and starts walking towards them. And so on. In our workshops this is then built up to the point where people run as fast as they can and shout the names as loud as they can. In this case there is more than one runner which means that people have to be incredibly alert and responsive. It also very quickly energises the group involved.

Our further spin on this is to establish sign names for each company or group member so that it is not the name of the individual that is called out but instead the person on the end of the eye contact gives back the person's sign name. By sign name, we mean a short gestural action that has been created in place of a verbal name. Like Sign Describe, this was inspired by findings during rehearsals for *On Blindness*. On day one Jenny Sealey, as Artistic Director for Graeae, set up a session where we all created a sign name for ourselves so that we might communicate with one another. This sign name was to conform to the conventions of BSL in that it involves the use of the hands and operates in a space in front of the chest area. Jenny suggested that we made our sign name personal to ourselves but within that there was total freedom as to what that might take the form of. It might be the way one was feeling that morning; it might be a physical characteristic or trait you are known for; it might be a representative action of your behaviour. We were encouraged to be creative and true to ourselves. To be creative meant that we were not pulled into the dark world of mime and the need to be true meant that it didn't have to be anything too elaborate. Each sign name should last only a few seconds and be clear, concise and repeatable.

Learning every sign name in the circle takes some time and every participant should be looking to emulate and copy the sign name in all its glory – this means not just getting the left and right details correct but also looking for rhythm, weight, momentum and details. We would normally treat this part of the exercise like a building block exercise, i.e. learn three or four and then go to the first person and run through them all before introducing another three or four. With each participant, once they have physically demonstrated their sign name and the group have a good grasp of it, ask the participant to say why they created the sign name that they did. This is also a useful way for people to remember every sign name once the exercise starts and begins to build momentum.

Like the traditional version, start the game at a slow, pedestrian pace as the group get used to responding to one another in this physical way. Once the group get the hang of it, encourage them to jog across the space and then build up a running speed. It is also useful to introduce the idea that the person being approached does not have to wait for the incoming person to be at their side before they themselves set off. As soon as they realise the correct response, they should set off into the space. The result of this is that the sign name they offer is an action that happens on the move. This is an interesting dynamic to observe.

If the group are confident working at full speed, then introduce a second person into the game. By this we mean that at any one time there are two people establishing eye contact and travelling across the space. This requires the group to make good use of their peripheral vision, as there is now double the rate of incidence and twice as many bodies crossing the same space at speed. In this version there is a strong chance, particularly with smaller numbers, that at times two people will find themselves converging on one individual. In this instance it is the responsibility of the two runners to recognise this and for one of them to switch their eye contact to another member of the circle at the last minute. This also requires the rest of the group to be extra alert too, in case they become a sudden choice by one of the two runners.

A development of this game is to introduce the spoken name along with the sign name. In this way, the game becomes a very, very simple exercise in combining words and movement. Any of the above versions are particularly useful when working with teams who are completely new to one another. It is surprising how often we have taught this exercise to university students four or five months into their course who have no idea what some of their fellow students are called.

MOVEMENT FOR NON-DANCERS/CHOREOGRAPHY THAT DOESN'T FEEL LIKE DANCE

Listed here are several task-based exercises that result in the creation of choreographed movement sequences without the group having to understand any of the basic tenets of choreography. Instead they take the form of tasks. By following a step-by-step approach, the cumulative effect is unapologetically choreographic without the participants having to think choreographically.

Chair Duets

This devising process keeps a large group busy with a fairly simple task. It is similar to and inspired by Hymns Hands (covered later and moving a little bit further into advanced territory) but is a group scene and captures a frenetic energy that, under your manipulation, can be comic and ultimately quite sad.

Chair Duets presents a very physical scene of touches, embraces, flirtations, rejections all played at a quite mesmerising speed. We have presented it as a sofa in a house that has seen the changing partners of all the people who have lived there. For it to work best we have found that it pays to withhold this information, this context, as it gets in the way of the participants achieving the speed this scene requires. If the task for them is just to achieve the choreography as fast and cleanly as they can, they will not get bogged down in acting the context. And they will need to know the moves extremely well to be able to take on the context later.

This works best with even numbers. Split your participants into groups of two and ask them to take chairs and find a space in the room where both chairs can sit side by side.

Try demonstrating the basic principle behind this. Two people sit on ordinary plastic or wooden chairs. They both face the front and remain seated. One of the partners is instructed to place a hand on the other. They can place this anywhere but the action must be firm and deliberate. (It is best to start simply so encourage them to use their partner's thighs and shoulders.) They should create approximately three moves, placing their own hands or moving the hands of their partner. They may choose to place these hands on themselves, their thighs, shoulders, knees, around their neck, or they may choose to place their partner's hands somewhere on the partner's own body. This might also include pushing their partner's torso forward or pulling them back into the chair. Once they have done this they remain in their final position and the other partner takes over. The same rules apply and then the original partner carries it on from the last position.

It is important to keep this simple and to make tiny, bite-sized chunks because they need to remember them and link them all together. It is also crucial to be on the look-out for a story being acted out. By that we mean look out for any attitude in the moves. Are they frustrated or flirtatious? Are they angry or petulant? Participants will generally try to give you more than you have asked for and more than you need. Remind them about the clarity of the task and the need to avoid *any* story.

Limit the couples to between 12 and 20 moves. (They can do more but it will impact on the overall running time of the final piece.) They should aim to achieve a smoothness in the transition of the hands and the transition between the partner that was leading and the partner that is taking over.

Now get the participants to keep practising this but avert their eyes from each other. Make them look out ahead and keep looking ahead. They need to remember these moves physically rather than visually.

Once they have grasped this and their moves are clean, fluid and fast, it is time to share the simple context. Tell them that what they are both looking out at is a television and they are both sitting on a sofa. They never take their eyes off the television and are oblivious to the touch and touching of their partners.

You can use a sofa but we stipulated chairs as we thought you were more likely to have them and it meant that everyone could rehearse at the same time. If you have a sofa, you could move the final piece to it once you have rehearsed on chairs. The advantage of making the work on chairs and not talking about the context is that you now have a very edgy and precise choreography to play with. This will contrast effectively with the lazy context. If you had placed your performers on the sofa and explained the couch potato context, then you might have had a job creating anything other than lazy choreography. Their physicality would have been the same as the context and would have effectively been saying the same thing twice.

You can run each pair's work to see how effectively they are managing to keep up the sharp physicality of the hands while still maintaining the couch potato physicality of the rest of the body and the focus on the television. It may take some rehearsing to achieve the mesmerising speed that is required.

To turn this into a group scene there are two ways to proceed:

First, number each pair and place everybody in a line so that the person in the left chair of couple 1 is next to the person in the right chair of couple 2. The person in the left chair of couple 2 is next to the person in the right chair of couple 3. Basically they are all in one line with no spaces between them. You are now going to work on the links that will turn this group of individual scenes into one piece of group choreography.

The person in the left chair of group 1 takes the person in the right chair of group 2 and makes a small version with them using the same techniques and focus as before. (It does not matter that they now know the context as they have been trained and know and have achieved the quality we are looking for.) Now that everyone has a new partner, pair up the remaining couple. This will be the person in the first chair at one end and the person in the last chair at the other. It is their new section that will allow the completed scene to loop if you want it to. If not, you can finish it with this new couple.

Once this stage is complete clear the room of all but one pair of chairs. These are the only chairs used in the scene. Everyone, apart from the first couple, is split into two groups – one in each wing. (For clarity, let's call the first couple group 1 and those in the wings groups 2 and 3.) Place group 1 in the chairs and get them to run their routine. Once complete the first person from group 2 runs on from the wings and needs to get rid of the person sat on the right-hand side of group 1 so that they can take their place and run their mini routine with their new partner from group 1. This expulsion of the redundant partner can be a brutal shove or swing off stage into the wings immediately followed by the new person sitting down and starting their mini routine. The same happens when the other half of the pair (from group 3) comes on and throws, pushes off the person from group 1 and starts their routine with their group 2 partner. The timing of the entrances should feel like an interruption and the couple in the chairs should not feel like they are waiting for someone to come along. This will take some mastering. It might help to go through the routine in front of the group and agree on what move the person running on is going to take as their signal. This helps emphasise how important clarity and consistency are as the moves have now become cues for people in the wings to run on stage. If they are not clear and consistent, then the person waiting in the wings will not get their cue.

Continue until the final couple get interrupted by the first person of group 1. (The whole thing can either loop or finish with the mini routine between the last person and the first from group 1.)

These transitions need to be swift but they can be creative and choreographed. You can either set time aside for this or just rely on the creativity of the whole group in the moment to offer suggestions or come up with new ideas.

Now that everything is in place it is time to reinforce the context. Remind everyone about the television and how their focus must never wander from it. Remind them how crisp the choreography must be to succeed.

Try the complete routine with a strong and upbeat music track. We have often used 'Lucky Star' by Basement Jaxx featuring Dizzee Rascal. The energy will lift the physicality and the urgency of the performers. We unashamedly time the run and then set a target of knocking another ten seconds off in the next run. Participants usually embrace this urgency and are desperate to know if they have succeeded in getting their time down (without compromising the quality of the work, of course).

The humour of the couples constantly changing, of old partners being dumped for new ones, starts to emerge. An evening or a lifetime of their possible cuddles and caresses flit by in a flash and then they are gone but nothing changes. The television and their fixation on it remains.

You still have the choice of whether you want to finish this scene with the last couple or with an individual alone. If you decide on someone alone, what do they do? Switch the television off? Then what? There is still the possibility of emotional impact in this scene despite its comedy and physicality. The end result can be quite moving. You can also play with the pace and physical dynamics to explore this. Try a slow run and ask the performers to maintain their gaze at the 'television'. How does this change the story or the tenderness between the couple?

We find this a very successful way of engaging a large group in a physical task that does not require previous physical experience and training. It is fun and is a really good way to focus the participants and get them committed to the success of the scene.

Get Ready

Get Ready was inspired by the preening and preparation that goes into a night out, looking at the differences between archetypal male and female behaviour. It was about the physicality of trying to catch your best side in the mirror, of the endless flicking and teasing of hair, of beauty tips and make-up sharing, excessive deodorant and random nasal hair pruning. It all takes place using and facing the audience as an imaginary mirror.

Get Ready was devised during the rehearsals for *Klub* and is developed here as a workshop/creative exercise. It is a particularly good exercise for beginners and those not normally given to devising physical material. By keeping the creative task simple but providing a strong performance focus, the exercise also hones basic performance skills that are essential to later exercises. In order to provide a firm basis for Get Ready, it is a good idea to choose a strong music track that has a steady and consistent 4/4 count. Though the size of each group can be flexible, three is probably the minimum you should have and a group that is too large will reduce the chance of everybody having an input into the creative part of the exercise. It is normally useful to split a full group into smaller groups of equal size. This is so that the productivity rate between each group in tackling the task has some chance of being equal, which makes for better time management when it comes to wrapping up the exercise and getting it to a performance or 'showing' level.

Each team places itself somewhere around the room in front of what is its fixed point of focus. This might be a poster, a fire alarm, a window opener – anything that sits at eye level to the group within the room. The group are to imagine this as their mirror. For the duration of the exercise, they are to use this as their point of focus rather than looking at themselves. Now they decide on whether they are to represent male or female characters. The instruction now is to create a string with the theme of getting ready in front of a mirror. It is helpful to set up the task with the thought that these preparations are for a big night out, where the preparatory activities might be more varied, exotic, detailed and flamboyant.

Depending on the ability of the group, they create a certain number of counts (8 or 16, for example, if the track to be worked with is in 4/4 time). The instruction might be for each individual to create such a string or for the group as a whole to create this. It is worth noting that, even with inexperienced and relatively new companies and groups, it is sometimes easier for them to create their own individual material, no matter how short, rather than trying to work collectively to create even a single bar of material. While the group are creating the material, use the chosen music track so that right from the start, each group has a sense of the tempo that they need to work to. Even if their sequence starts out at a much slower pace as they begin to construct it, it is helpful to have the tempo set out from the start and the track playing throughout the devising period.

In using counts and a heavy tempo, there is often the tendency to create heavy material. This is where, over a count of eight, the string consists of four actions with each action landing on an even count and the group using the odd counts to move from one position to another. It is also often in tandem with very symmetrical movement choices, e.g. right hand goes on right hip, left hand goes on left hip, look at face in profile on the right side, look at face in profile on the left side. This is a very natural response of groups not used to working with counts. It is very easily developed into something far more interesting. Once the string has been made, ask the group to break the regularity of the pattern, even if this is just by stretching out a single move. We often criticise groups for making material where their next move is something we on the outside knew was going to happen. Ask the group to experiment with the rhythm so they avoid the heaviness of a string that plays out one TWO three FOUR five SIX seven EIGHT. Instead, they might play out a string where the heavy, landed moments might be one TWO three four five SIX SEVEN EIGHT where the lowercase numbers are where the group are moving through and into positions and the uppercase numbers are hitting what might best be described as the finished poses. A count structure like the latter one here will be more interesting purely because it sets up quite a calm start and finishes with a flurry of activity, confounding expectation and rhythmic second guessing.

Once each group has created their string, the basic set-up to observe the work is to ask each group to step out of their imagined space. From these newfound 'side lines', the group are to add an eight count onto the front of their material, which is the time they will then take to enter their space from their side line and establish their positions in front of their mirror. Allow each group around the room to play out their own version of the exercise with their individual group mirrors.

For a slightly more choreographed whole, establish a single mirror somewhere in the eye line that all groups now use as their focus point. Split the groups to either side of this central focus point as far as the room will allow, then give each group a number, putting the odd numbered groups on one side of the room and the evens on the other. Now run the exercise using each group in turn to create a collective sequence, with each team crossing into the space over eight counts, hitting a central position in front of the single, collective mirror before running through their string. Variants to play with at this stage include asking the groups to exit to the opposite side of the space once they have completed their string. Another is for the entering group to use the same eight counts as the group that are exiting. This crossover moment is good for testing group spatial awareness.

In terms of performance techniques, add in scenarios such as the idea that this is now the mirror of a public bathroom. See what implications this creates for the material and the way in which it is executed. A further instruction would be for the group to imagine that this public bathroom is prohibitively small and they must jostle for space. Following this instruction, the groups should look to adapt their material in order to convey the truth of the new scenario. An additional suggestion might be that these are reluctant party people who wish they were doing anything else instead. Perhaps the mirror is a bedroom mirror and, in providing privacy, allows the individuals to scrutinise themselves and possibly doubt the process of making themselves beautiful or attractive.

Alternatively, they may start out timid and become newborn in the process, a paragon of confidence.

A further development is to create a freeform Get Ready where a few or possibly even all the groups self-orchestrate by making their own choices as to when they enter and leave the space/mirror. By self-orchestration, we mean an exercise where the participating group are constantly in control of the rhythm and rate of incidence within the exercise, making continuous choices as to how the scenario is playing out. A successful Get Ready should play with notions of populating the space. A continuously full room soon becomes lacking in focus and interest. So does a room with nobody in it.

A final advancement is to start cutting into the string itself. Encourage group members to stop treating the string as a sequential number of events. (It might be useful here not to use the track that the groups have been working to. A slightly more ambient track or one without a strong count structure will encourage them to be freer with the material.) Instead, the gestural material is to be cut into – maybe a single move is repeated, half achieved, reversed. It might take a whole minute to complete only the first two moments from the original string. The whole sequence might be played out in a few frenzied seconds. Play with the pace of the moves. If the exercise involves more than one group, begin to play with picking up on other people's material, creating ripples and echoes of movement around the group. Stillness and mid-action pauses should also be encouraged to see what effect they bring. Again, it might be interesting to throw in suggestions that enhance the performances, particularly by suggesting various emotional states that the group might find themselves in. The group should always be observant, particularly from the side lines, in order to self-orchestrate and experiment with what provides most interest. At all times we should believe that there is a mirror which the entire group are working from and in. (It is always useful to have some of the group out front as an audience as they can pick up on all the accidental connections.)

Play with how the performing group are presented. By drawing curtains and making a small aperture though which they are glimpsed by the audience, it is possible to present the idea of a mirror. The mirror then becomes something the audience can see through yet the protagonists appear unaware of the observers. This can give the scene a voyeuristic feel.

Get Ready takes a very simple idea as a starting point and asks participants to draw on familiar language that can be playful and quick to create. Mixing up males and females within groups is as valid as having groups of single sexes. The inclusion of the mirror means that the intention of the exercise/scene is always apparent. The further versions of Get Ready mentioned here are also very useful starting points in considering group dynamics and ensemble performance.

Ways into basic lifting techniques

There is something absurd about trying to tackle this within a book, but it seemed even more wrong to ignore it. So here it goes . . .

Getting people lifting is a careful process. There are all kinds of preconceptions, hang-ups, fears and concerns to overcome. Make sure everyone is warmed up as they are all going to be working their backs, arms and legs. It would be good to start by playing a game of Clear the Space (see page 114) as the 'Person' command gets people gripping, holding and embracing each other without a thought for decorum or protocol. Such abandon or ease with physical proximity is crucial before you start working on lifts as people will have to be able to relax into their partner and not recoil away.

Then there are the preconceptions. Many people may consider a lift between two people to be an act of strength – one person imposing their strength upon another more passive person. The kind of lifting we would recommend does not necessarily require strength. It is mostly about simple technique.

Even though it is impossible for us to demonstrate physically from within these pages there are certainly some rules that will stand you in good stead. This list is probably not exhaustive.

1   Get your core lower than that of the person you are lifting. Basic principles of martial arts like Judo are all about using and controlling your partner's or adversary's weight from this position.
2   If you are being lifted, do not deny your partner your weight. Give it to them freely. Do not push away. Pull in. If anything, push down on or into them. And think about going up, about the lift succeeding, not all the ways it could fail.
3   Don't look down at your feet. They won't go anywhere with you looking at them.
4   If you are using strength, then you are not using technique. Lifting can be more about positioning and balance than brute force.
5   Be safe. Do not over-rehearse. Do not be over-ambitious.
6   Don't forget to breathe. Holding your breath freezes the back muscles you need to be active. Exhale slowly with control if you are catching.
7   Think 'rucksack'! Let us explain . . .

Everyone can imagine a cradle lift: Picture lifting a baby, or the way a muscle-bound hero might emerge from a burning building in a Hollywood film carrying the beautiful heroine. That is the preconception we need to fight. If possible, get a couple to replicate this image. It will be hard work for the lifter so make sure the people demonstrating are safe and capable.

Now encourage the person being lifted to be active: Get them to pull their weight into their partner, putting their arms around the shoulders of the lifter. Ask them to bring their knees up to their chest, engaging their stomach muscles in doing so. They should put their head on the lifter's shoulder and make themselves as small and all tightly packaged as possible to get as close to their partner as they can.

Now talk to the lifter. Can they take their arms away? Can they literally wear their partner around their shoulder? Can they walk and turn as if they are just wearing some enormous human scarf? If so, then the 'lift' has become the work of the lifted and they are being worn just like a rucksack. They are no longer passive or like a fainting heroine in *Gone with the Wind*. They are now active and working with the lifter.

This is an extreme but effective example of how much work is involved in being lifted. It is also an example of how easy lifting can be if the lifted partner is active and the weight is placed in the right place.

Working with lifts is a practical exercise and cannot be dictated by books, but what we hope to have offered are some simple rules that can open up and simplify a way of working that can seem far too ambitious and frightening.

NEW PHYSICAL VOCABULARY/RESTRICTIONS AND FREEDOM

The following exercises are designed to bring surprising choreographic qualities out of your performers. They will test them, sometimes close to the point of meltdown, but what will emerge is a kind of physicality that might be impossible to achieve were it not for the intense demands of these exercises.

Sell Out Floor/Caterpillar

The following exercises are considered advanced only in that they both bypass the act of creating actual choreography. Instead, both use an existing string of material as the starting point. Sell Out Floor was developed for the penultimate scene in *Sell Out* while Caterpillar takes its name from the Keoki track which was placed halfway through the performance of *Hymns*. Both exercises follow a similar idea that will become evident as you read on. In both cases, we outline specific choreographic ideas as starting points, ones which were specific to each show. Of course this can be adapted as seen fit. We specify it here only in an attempt to be as clear as possible about the process rather than the actual result we created. Following these exercises to the letter, however, does serve as a great opportunity for practitioners to adapt existing material and create constructive constrictions that challenge the workings of the body.

For Sell Out Floor, arrange the group into either pairs or small teams – three or four per team is possible but pairs are preferable; any more than this might be too difficult. From here, get the participants to create a simple fight sequence with each other using grips, lifts and throws. At this stage there is no need to work at full speed. What is important is to create a string of events that embody aggression, with bodies locked in combat that remains upright for the most part. In rehearsals for the show, our choreographer T. C. Howard was interested in an accentuated physical dynamism for this sequence. In order to achieve this, we created the piece wearing heavy-duty jackets that allowed each of us to take hold of and throw our partners across the space and into the air. The heavy-duty nature of the clothing meant that the performer had slightly more padding than usual and also the ability to grip was made easier, creating a better 'fling' capacity and making it easier to lift and slam one another. We also discussed the ways in which dogs fight. This was noted as involving lots of pinning to the floor, particularly with one partner face down on the floor and the victor on top exerting pressure.

The next level requires all participants to have good knowledge of the sequence. Basically, each person reruns the material but this time as a solo, imagining the partner to be locked in with them so following all the existing dynamics of weight, tempo, swings, landings and impacts. This might take some time. Remembering the sequence itself is not such a difficult task. Investing it with the same movement quality is.

Next, ask the practitioners to lie face up on the floor and now try to re-appropriate the same sequence as when they were standing. At this stage, it is important to work slowly through some sections as the task of recreating some of the movement will require some extensive contortions of the body. This is time very well spent: The body needs thinking time to co-ordinate positions that, while not impossible, are likely to be very alien.

The result for *Sell Out* was one of our most long-standing favourite sequences. Movements such as leaping back in the initial devising session became dynamic salmon-like flips away from the surface of the floor. Simple moves of the head and shoulders while standing created incredibly fast revolves on the floor. Over time even these unnatural contortions became possible at incredibly high speeds. The use of the clothing specified above meant that in moments where we did connect, we were able to keep the energy levels of the sequence up by way of almost superhuman flings of the adversarial body through the air or into the ground. The fact that the floor sequence remained true to the standing version also meant that the sequence still retained real clarity of meaning despite the physical and therefore visual contortions of the material. Arguably, the distorted nature of this new material gave much support to the idea that here were four people wrestling with their internal demons as much as with one another.

Caterpillar is a solo exercise and, for the purposes of *Hymns*, the material was based around a set that consisted of four golden ladders that ran to the height of the theatre. Having ladders to work with does make for great material but this does not mean that a similar exercise could not be undertaken simply by placing participants in front of a wall space. Any bar-like structure in a gymnasium would also be a useful start to the exercise in terms of creating the initial material. For us, the ladders were an obvious metaphor for the idea of the career ladder (the show concerned itself with four male twentysomething characters) and also an allusion to the story of Jacob's ladder (the four men being brought together by the death of a mutual friend).

Set the task of creating material that is based around the idea of trying (unsuccessfully) to scale the ladder. The vocabulary should be one of leaps, grasps, falls, misses, swings and occasional catches. As stated earlier, the use of something like a ladder is useful here though, if memory serves well, the presence of the actual ladder does render the exercise rather painful on the hands after a while. Any near misses might mean a collapse to the ground – a moment which might lead to some activity on the floor, gearing the body up for another onslaught in the attempt to leave the ground behind and ascend the rungs.

Once there is a set string of good, full-blooded material in place, the next stage in the exercise is to invert the space. All the material that existed on the ladder or wall surface is now transferred to the floor and similarly any floor material now takes place at the face of the ladder or wall surface. As with Sell Out Floor, this stage of the exercise should be given adequate time and concentration while practitioners attempt to accommodate the new playing area. The floor obviously restricts movement that was made freely in an upright standing position but this in itself needs to be made a virtue, using the floor as a surface to be played against. In the same way, floor-bound material should not suddenly become wild and free just because the spatial limitations have been expanded. Upright material should adhere to the same physical principles discovered while lying on the floor.

This exercise was incredibly refreshing during *Hymns* rehearsals. With particular reference to the task of transferring the floor-made material into the upright state, the ways in which our bodies wrapped themselves around the ladders was of a form that we would never have discovered had the material been made in any other way. Asking the floor material to suddenly engage with the ladder structure was occasionally very challenging and at certain times there had to be concessions made, but even such concessions gave rise to physical material that felt truly innovative and far more challenging than anything that might have come through simply launching ourselves at the set in the conventional manner.

Both Caterpillar and Sell Out Floor, as exercises in manipulating the playing plane, require participants to be fairly diligent and detailed in their approach to physical work. It is all too easy to simply follow an easy route with such exercises rather than really challenge the body to repeat the same material once the goal posts have not just moved but turned themselves into a picket fence. Both offer fantastic opportunities to drop the 'bag of tricks' inherent in all our bodies and discover a new vocabulary. Yet with such simple shifts, the theatrical context is not obliterated. Instead, it remains intact while the physical response remains both true and innovative – a point at which you might just have reached pure theatrical nirvana, then?

Dirty Ballroom

This exercise was used in the making of *Dirty Wonderland* for a final scene that took place in the vast ballroom of the Grand Ocean Hotel in Saltdean near Brighton. Choreographically, it attempts to create something that is almost familiar and relevant to the immediate environment but not quite. It also challenges the performers' ability to coordinate their upper bodies with their legs and feet and requires a solid understanding of counts in order to alleviate some of the tensions and difficulties inherent in the creation of material using this method. (Note: In the creation of Dirty Ballroom, one of our most experienced dancers felt compelled to cry out 'Oh, you're f***ing joking . . .' when given the task.)

Cait Davis, in *Dirty Wonderland*, 2005

Set the performers the task of creating a sequence that involves only legs and feet. Ask them to set it to counts, e.g. create two bars of material. While working on this, ask the performers to have their arms folded at all times. In this way, any material they create with the bottom half should have no effect on their top half. For our show we asked our team to create a foot pattern that was 'something like ballroom' but was not identifiable as any existing form of ballroom dancing. Other suggestions for material might be the stepping patterns and shapes involved when trying on a brand new pair of shoes (an idea that we tried out briefly during the making of *Market Boy*), the mechanics of moving through snow, the unconscious patterns we create when bored, anxious, desperate for the toilet, etc. (For a long time now we have been desperate to create a sequence based on the fantastic moves we create with our feet on discovering we have just stepped in a gargantuan dog deposit. The material is all there; it's just that we have yet to find a show in which such material is necessary. Who knows, it might turn out to be the most charming entrance for Othello . . .)

Once this material has been created it is important to ensure that it is tied strictly to a count that is clear, concise and repeatable and that the movement exists only in the lower half of the body.

Next, set the task of creating a separate sequence that involves just the arms. We have found that, in order to get the best results, this session should be undertaken at a later date so that the performers do not make the link between the two strings of material. For *Dirty Wonderland*, we spent a morning watching clips of 50's swimming star Esther Williams in films such as *Easy to Love* and *Million Dollar Mermaid*. In particular, the company were asked to pay close attention to the arms and the quality of movement employed by Esther. Following this, the company all sat in chairs and were asked to create a sequence using only arms that in some way referred to the style used in the film clips we had seen. Other ideas for creating this type of material might be the movement of hands and arms during moments of anxiety, the simple task of preparing your clothes and/or hair, the actions involved in trying to create warmth for yourself. While working on *Black Watch* for the National Theatre of Scotland, one session looked specifically at the kinds of movements associated with the stiffening of limbs after spending hours sat within the confines of an armoured vehicle with temperatures of 140 degrees Fahrenheit. Again, this material should be memorised in a way that is clear, concise and repeatable and exists within a firm count structure. To make the next part easier, both feet and arms sequences should be set within the same number of counts.

The final part of this exercise involves putting the two sequences together, top half alongside bottom half. In restricting the impact of the legs on the upper body by folding arms and similarly restricting the effects of the arms on the lower body by being seated during the creation of the arms sequence, the outcome of this exercise can be rather tricky to execute. It is likely that, in combining the two strings of material, the resultant sequence has no natural physical sense through the body. Weight and its emphasis shifts around the body in ways not normally executed. The results often involve weird twists and contortions, ways of moving that we would not have thought of without these constraints. The use of a strong count structure is essential as, at this stage, it is the only element that unifies top and bottom in an understandable way.

This part of the exercise might take some time. The important thing here is to remain true to the sequences as they existed in isolation and not to let the counts or moves slide slightly in order to create moments that feel like they 'make sense'. Chances are that, in doing this, we revert back to known ways of moving which defeats the whole object of the exercise.

In *Dirty Wonderland* the resulting scene involved 30 dancers in unison. The surrounding ballroom provided all the context we required while the sequence itself looked like no traditional form of ballroom known to humankind. By carefully selecting the impetus behind creating the material, we were able to create a whole new form of movement that had no moment that one might identify as being part of the foxtrot, for instance, but at all times made total sense of the opulent surroundings that the ballroom gave us.

For us, this exercise was used in a very specific way in order to provide a sequence for a very specific scene. In listing the possibilities of other ideas, we are pointing out how this exercise might be useful in creating sequences for shows that cover a whole range of themes and events. However, this exercise is also useful in itself and one idea might be to create top- and bottom-half material that bears no relation to each other at all. In combining the two strings, this exercise is a great opportunity to unlock the physical restrictions inherent in our habitual physicality. It also doesn't allow us to use our 'bag of tricks' when moving.

It is worth pointing out that the combining part of this exercise can take a long time and needs practitioners to apply themselves to the exercise over what might be a considerable amount of time. Part of our job during rehearsals for *Dirty Wonderland* while making this sequence was listening out for the groans and yells of exasperation as various members of the cast lost their will to live! At times such as this, one or both of us would be on hand to mop up the bits of brain that would inevitably be seeping out of the ear of the hapless performer. In extreme cases, the words 'tea break' are always useful.

This process is certainly a challenge and a commitment but well worth it as it produces a movement quality that would be impossible to achieve outside of the task.

ADVANCED EXERCISES – PUSHING THE POTENTIAL

Here are a number of exercises for the more advanced practitioner that require some choreographic experience. The level of experience of the person or people running the exercise does not matter as long as the instructions are made clear and the participating group are observed closely.

Hymns Hands

Hymns Hands is our name for a very simple and effective choreographic technique introduced to us by Liam Steel and used by him in *Hymns*. We have since taken on and developed this technique and use it to show the flexibility of choreography and to demonstrate how that choreography meets context to create meaning. This exercise also explores how important the audience are in defining that meaning.

Split the participants into groups of two. Get them to stand opposite their partners. One of the partners places their hands firmly on the other, or manipulates their partner's hands, placing them on their own body. They can also place their partner's hands on the partner's body.

Once they place a hand it has to stay there. The contact must be firm and secure. The palm must press into the flesh. The fingertips should be sensitised.

Each partner should take turns placing their partner's or their own hands on their bodies. Allow each partner to be in control for between two and four moves before control switches to the other partner. They start from where the first partner finished.

Remember to instruct them to think of bite-sized chunks. This exercise is going to be hard to remember so do a little bit and return to the beginning after every couple of additions. This may seem unnecessary but it is methodical. These moves can be forgotten so quickly, particularly the latest additions.

Avoid touching the head. Avoid one person's palms touching the palms of the other. Avoid purposely weird shapes. Avoid any sense of story or attitude. It is so easy for a move to start saying 'I hate you!' You need the moves to be pure choreography because it is precisely the meaning of these moves that we are going to explore later. It is extremely useful for the group to see the moves simply as moves at this stage. They can then see how we can invest them with complex meaning later.

Each couple should aim to have a slick and well-practised string of between 12 and 20 moves. Once they have this get them to find a way from the last move into the first move, effectively creating a loop of material. This link should be an additional move entirely in keeping with the style and quality of the work created so far.

Invite the pairs to show their work to the rest of the group. See how fast and slick they can get it, taking care to iron out the minute pauses that tend to exist in the moments where control switches from one partner to the other. This is how they achieve fluidity.

Even at this stage results can be impressive.

There is an interesting experiment you could insert at this point. Get one of the couples to demonstrate and, midway through their string, tell them to shut their eyes. Their initial response might be confusion and lack of confidence, but if you push them to keep going they can start to display what looks like a remarkable physical intuition! After a while they may even be faster than with their eyes open. Even if they are not, the exercise reminds them that there is a mental and physical understanding between the partners. They do know the material. They can remember what it feels like rather than what it looks like. This is a crucial step as performers have to have this physical muscle memory with their moves before they are ready to start adding words. Only then can the words and moves exist together with differing dynamics. Only then can they (the words and the movement) comment on each other rather than reiterate what each other is saying. We would suggest that this is the successful approach to marrying words with movement. If the words and movement share the same dynamic and rhythm, then you are in danger of saying the same thing twice and battering your audience around the head with meaning.

Now that we have appreciated the moves and have acknowledged that they have no meaning in themselves, we can start playing with story.

Place a couple in the middle of the room. Name them A and B. Get them to practise their moves again. Once they are secure with them get a third volunteer from the rest of the group. This third person, C, has to walk around the room constantly looking into B's eyes. They can play with proximity but they should keep it fairly simple too.

B must always look for C. They must always try to maintain eye contact throughout.

A always looks at B.

The difficulty is now being able to fulfil your moves while you are looking at a person who continually moves around the room. C may be behind A; they could be far away; they could be just behind B. B must twist their head and eyes to always be in contact but not alter their physical routine with A.

Play with music here. Your choice can set the tone of the story that emerges.

Ask the rest of the group what story is emerging. They may have differing takes on it, but what usually emerges is a complex love triangle where B is having their head turned by the attention of C and A is oblivious to it all. Or A is stoically carrying on, desperately trying to regain their partner's attention. B is going through the motions with their relationship but has mentally already left.

Depending on the music this can be slightly comic or utterly tragic. The point is that a complex story has started to emerge. It is the kind of complexity that would take ages to write.

It should be pointed out that any story that has emerged has come to be through the addition of the direction and the music to the choreography. The choreography never sought to encapsulate this story.

We could take this story further. Returning to our 'love trio', what would happen if B breaks off from A to follow C, leaving A to carry on doing the moves without their partner? Is A now in denial of the breakup or are they consciously trying to get through it and maintain some dignity? Now that their moves don't physically connect are they seeking out that physical contact or are they trying to remember what it felt like?

Thrust this upon the couple unexpectedly. Talk to them as they are doing their moves and insist B escapes. This will leave an embarrassed and struggling A. Don't let them off the hook – keep at them, asking them to keep going, find their way through it. They should not give up and laugh or acknowledge their predicament with those watching, but the struggle of them trying to remember the moves is all part of the theatricality.

Leave them to struggle but keep talking to them. As they get better at remembering it, does their dignity and strength return?

Ask them to make the moves smaller. Talk to them about the memory of the moves fading away. The moves are now a trace version. What does this tell us from the outside?

Alternatively, keep A doing their moves and ask B to fluidly find their way back into the moves. They might do this while looking back to C and then allow that eye contact to fade and their focus to return to A. They can continue their moves. How do we feel about this? Is B welcomed back? Is the affair over?

We are now playing with and manipulating a story. And there are always two sides to every story, so . . .

Try this: Set the couple up as before – A with B and B obsessed with C. While B is following C around the room with their eyes, instruct A to leave and B to continue with the moves. B still has to watch C and is oblivious to the fact that A has left. What if C leaves? Do B's moves become redundant? Do they fade? Is B now alone?

The outcome of the story has changed. Is it the other side of the coin? Has this story become moralistic? The point is how flexible and rich the scenario is. And it is such simple choreography.

You can play with the physicality itself, as well as the context. Try stretching a moment of physicality. Allow it to have a completely different rhythm and dynamic to the moves that surround it. Think of the bullet-time effect in the film *The Matrix* and similar oft-used special effects in numerous Chinese martial arts films.

Now take another couple and get them to rehearse their moves. Once they are confident change the dynamic slightly. Now they have to move very slowly and deliberately through their string of material. The touch needs to be very firm. The placing of hands has to be secure and deliberate. The hand has to really press into the flesh.

Both partners have to watch each hand on its journey towards the other partner's body and through to the completion of the move. They then both intently watch the next move, and so on. Prime them to look up at each member of the group watching on your command. Tell them to be confident and really look into the eyes of each one while maintaining the quality of the moves.

Place them far away from the rest of the group. Try taking the group out of the room to a place where they can only peer through a window or can only partially see the couple. Try a fairly slow and sparse piece of music, e.g. 'Skym' by Underworld. How does this affect the audience? Do they feel voyeuristic? And what about the moves: Do they have a different intensity and meaning? And the music? (We often note that this situation makes the people watching breathe in a different way! This is a response to the music, the uncertainty of the new context, the personal tenderness of the moves.)

Bring the audience back into the room. Get them closer to the couple. Does this change things?

Give the couple the instruction to look up at the audience. Let the instruction be a simple word agreed before you start the exercise. How does this change things for the audience? What if you now make the audience retreat to their distant position?

We often get people talking about the burgeoning sexuality between the characters. Note that the performers have now become characters! People might talk about how they watched every move in minute detail, noting that the focus has changed from the previous couple. People might mention the way they felt they were intruding upon something. They might mention the way the characters challenged them to judge, or not judge their love, how the atmosphere changed from tender to provocative.

There may be lots of differing takes on the observers' experience. Of course you can't usually move your audience around like that in a performance, but the point is that what we have watched is still in the rehearsal room. We are still learning what is the best way to present our work and the audience's experience should be taken into consideration.

There is another exercise that can demonstrate how simple it can be to create completely different meanings from identical choreography just through slight contextual adjustments.

Stockholm Bed

This exercise has been developed from some early improvisations on the *Stockholm* project. It has moved on slightly from the original brief and is now used mostly as an illustrative example of the way movement can be manipulated to tell different stories. This has been explored in detail above (Hymns Hands), but this exercise is so simple and immediately effective that it is well worth a try.

Version 1

You don't need a bed. Place a couple on the floor and set everyone else back to watch. A can manipulate a supine B. They can turn them over, squeeze them up into a ball, hold them tightly, etc. They can take moments of rest where they just cuddle or place their head on B. They can also have a moment of thought where they just sit and look at B. (It does not matter what this thought is. It just needs to be a moment of stillness. It is this moment that your audience will leap into and project meaning upon.)

B keeps their eyes closed and allows themselves to be moved wherever A wishes. The movement can be gentle with rolls and stretches. It should be tender and intimate.

Georgina Lamb and Samuel James make up in *Stockholm*, 2007

This can be an improvisation and they do not have to set the moves. This means that they can demonstrate it to the group straightaway.

Choose a suitable piece of music to complement this intimacy, making sure the performers treat it as aural wallpaper and not as something emotionally instructive.

The responses might suggest a story of a lover tending an ill partner. It might be very moving. Ask about the moment of stillness. What was going through the mind of A?

Version 2

Take the couple aside and give them new instructions. Ask them to replicate the movement as they remember it. They do not have to get it perfect. It just has to feel like the moves from the first version. This time B must look at A all of the time, no matter where A places them. B must try to keep their eyes on A. A does almost exactly what they did in the first version, including the moment of stillness or thought. A major difference this time is that B will want to say something but can't get it out. B has a growing panic and frustration. A will try to calm B down through pressure and caress. A must try to reassure B with their hugs and squeezes.

Choose your music carefully now. Something slightly off kilter and quietly unnerving might help, but otherwise make sure it does not dwarf the couple. If in doubt, use the same music as in version 1.

Now what are the 'audience' responses? What tends to transpire here is a much more disturbing scenario. A's love is now smothering, sinister, and frightening; B appears to be in real peril. Is this abuse of a disabled person? Is this Stephen King's *Misery*?

The results can be genuinely disturbing. And all we have really done is ask B to open their eyes and watch A throughout. These little touches change everything from general atmosphere to specific meaning. The little adjustments have redefined how we read love, from tender and protective, to potentially sadistic and predatory.

The lesson, as ever, is that the choreography itself did not possess the meaning. We have played with the potential meanings all around the choreography. The performers facilitated the manipulation of the audience, as did the music and their proximity to the action. The story is the effect of this manipulation and the audience's response.

Again, we learn from this and then harness and take ownership of the best results.

In the *Stockholm* research and development sessions we took this a little further. We played with what it was that B wanted to say. In one run we brought the music down to reveal what was being said. When it became clear that B was asking to be allowed to go to the toilet and A was just hushing them and pressing down on them, the full horror of the sadism was revealed.

The next run had A walking away from B as they lay on the floor. We brought the music down to reveal B shouting about how they were not ready to stop yet and that A should come back! This turned everything on its head in the final seconds. It changed smothering sadism into a potentially sexual sado-masochism. It was an exciting example of giving an audience part of a story, inviting them to jump in with both feet and then giving the story a little twist to let the audience know they might have got it all wrong.

This was particularly relevant for *Stockholm* as it was about an abusive couple who might be our friends. The relationship might look very different from the inside than it does to us on the outside. We were at pains to find ways in which it would become difficult to judge them from the outside with any certainty. This uncertainty was crucial to the success of *Stockholm*.

Devising choreography for site-specific theatre

How do you set up a conducive environment when aiming to create site-specific physical work? There are probably many ways of tackling this, just as there are many kinds of site-specific theatre. In this section we are going to concentrate on the creation of highly physical choreography that aims to incorporate the limitations and opportunities unique to your specific site. So here is . . .

One way of doing it

Get your performers initiated into the space. Examine. Play. Experience it. Look for ledges and shelves. They are looking for areas where they can achieve some kind of purchase to get themselves off the floor. What are the dynamic possibilities of this space? What can they physically achieve?

In addition, simply spend some moments with them walking the space or using it naturalistically. This is not only good for observing their natural behaviour within this environment (remember that this can offer a lot of creative inspiration and physical material in itself) but also serves as a health and safety fact-finding mission. It is a risk assessment by the people who are going to be taking the physical risks.

There may be a downside to this, though. This approach may get your performers thinking only about the limitations of the space rather than the opportunities it provides. This outcome should be avoided at all costs. To help with this, there is . . .

Another way of doing it

For a start it is not always possible to have the 'site' at your disposal from day one of rehearsal. This does not mean that you cannot embark on incredibly fruitful groundwork. Of course, as the director/choreographer, it really helps to have a good understanding of the site and of ultimately what you want to achieve in there. Importantly we stress 'achieve' rather than 'choreograph'. We think the former is more open to inspiration and input from your collaborators and performers. It suggests a bar that, ideally, you want everyone to help you raise.

What follows are the early stages of development based on a two-day site-specific workshop set in the function room of a pub. The workshop was intended for professional practitioners but the lessons learnt are useful for practitioners of all levels of ability looking to make site-specific work.

Stage 1

Work on basic lifting techniques. Never underestimate how little your performers might know about safely lifting and being lifted. (One of the first things you need to tackle is the perceived notions about the roles of the lifted and the lifter. See 'Ways into basic lifting techniques', page 148.)

It is really important to get your participants confident in moving each other around. This can be tackled in many different ways. On this occasion we concentrated on a squeezing technique where both partners are active. While the 'lifter' gets their core lower than their partner's, the 'lifted' is thinking about climbing, pressing down into their partner. This keeps the weight close to the 'lifter's' core and much easier to manipulate.

Stage 2

Explore how you can now move your partner through the space. Give the lift a direction that is not simply up and down. Play with making this as effortless as possible. The key is always for the 'lifter' to aim for a point of balance where they can take their partner's weight as if it were a rucksack, positioned in such a way that the weight of the 'lifted' is falling through their own core.

Focus on where you want to get to. Look at this point when you move. Don't get immersed in the body you are lifting. This emphasis on focus will help give the moves direction.

Stage 3

Encourage the 'lifted' to become more active. A twist of the hips during a lift may allow them to come back to the ground in a position of strength, instantly ready to swap roles and take the weight of their partner. The key to becoming more adept at this swap is to always be thinking about the logic of the *next* move. This will become apparent through steady exploration, but the improved delivery of such moves is all about knowing where you need to be next and having the confidence to take your weight from one move into the place it needs to be for the next move without returning to a neutral stance.

Take plenty of time over this stage. This is where accidents can happen and it is also the most demanding stage so far, not just physically but mentally. This is the first time partnerships face failure and it is important to be able to help them through it and keep an eye on what it is that might be holding them back. (Most problems relate back to the perceived roles of the 'lifter' and the 'lifted'. It is another reason why we like to break things down into simple stages or building blocks. When problems occur there is always a simple lesson to refer to.)

Stage 4

The couples should now have a string of material – lifts and shunts that propel each other across the room. This should be safely set. It is important to set strings such as these as they act as building blocks in themselves.

Have a look at the set material. Encourage the partners to now aim for something more extreme, to be bigger, to cover more ground horizontally. They are to use their set material and adapt it. (This means that your request for something more demanding and dynamic does not lead to something reckless and utterly without the inherent safety measures put in place so far.)

It might be useful to workshop some of the couples in front of the rest of the group. See how they respond to encouragement and praise while letting them know that you want more. What you are aiming for here is the kind of apparent abandon in the way weight is transferred from one to the other. In reality, of course, there is no such abandon. It is just that they know what they are doing. They just don't look like they have to think about it any more.

This, in itself, is a major achievement whether you are working with young students or seasoned professionals, but it is still only a building block. Flushed with success you are about to challenge them in a way they would not be ready for if you had not taken them through the preceding stages.

Stage 5

Put participants into groups of three. Explain that now you want them to achieve the same thing as before but in a group of three.

Look out for them trying to execute lifts that mean there is always a spare body standing by, waiting to be involved in the next move. Similarly, watch out for two people lifting a passive and confused third person.

It is this passivity of the 'lifted' that you really have to address here. Get your groups to retain all of what they have learnt so far but to think about the task differently. Encourage the person at the back of the three to 'climb' the others, to commit to a move and let the other two adapt and position themselves in the best place to receive the moving weight. The two 'lifters' must safely place the 'lifted' to the floor and all three must quickly prepare for their new roles that will see one of them become the 'climber'.

They are aiming for a secure fluidity in the transference of weight and roles. It should result in bodies appearing to tumble through the air rather than merely appearing to be lifted. Each time, the 'lifted' has to think about what they can use to move their body. Rather than being manhandled by the 'lifters', they are using the bodies beneath them, treating the 'lifters' as ledges and shelves. The lifters are helping provide those ledges and shelves and helping to keep the whole thing fluid and safe.

When they are starting to achieve this they should be encouraged to attack the moves, to provide them with energy. What you ideally want to see is an apparently instinctive relationship develop between 'lifter' and 'lifted'. You don't want to be able to see them thinking about it.

Stage 6

Once you have achieved all of this work on physical trust, confidence and technique, you might remind your performers to think about the space. Point out that in the previous stage of the process you explored ledges and shelves. These could just as easily have been desks, tables, chairs or work surfaces. Now encourage them to return to the space and see those ledges and shelves as opportunities to interact with their surroundings.

Allow the groups of three to explore what they can now do in the space, using each other as lifters and the ledges etc. wherever they appear to offer help.

It is very important to have all of the stages of the process in mind even at this late stage. If the physical interaction and quality of the movement appears to be dissipating, then you can quickly refer to one of the previous stages to pull things back on track. It is very easy to lose the plot by trying to do too much and forgetting all of the important things you have learnt along the way. Hopefully, adhering to this process means that you always have something simpler to refer to and help you through the more complex task.

Site-specific theatre and the video camera

Being out of the theatre gives you an immediate literal context to play with. The hardest part is getting your target audience to see the work in the way that you saw it. Achieving an equality of experience for your audience can be very difficult. Of course, some companies thrive on this inequality and intend to offer radically different experiences of the work for different members of the audience. We appreciate the value of this, but it was something we wanted to avoid in making *Dirty Wonderland*, our only site-specific show so far.

Often when we are running advanced physicality workshops we introduce the idea of making work for the camera. This is a very different process and has its own demands. The biggest difference is that we are all working to perform for one vision, one perspective. There is no-one else but the camera and everything out of shot does not exist. This framing is very useful. It means that we don't have to worry about what happens out of shot. It is all about what is in the frame. It means you can achieve a lot of things that were impossible if you were performing in front of an audience. (You can also have several takes, if it goes wrong!)

Creating physical work for the camera is a good way of focusing the group you are working with. The results are immediate and visible for all and most young people would be intrigued to see themselves on a TV screen. It is easy for them to evaluate the success of the work and to see where it can improve. If you factor in these sessions looking at the 'rough cuts', you might find that the need to return to the work and get it right is now not an issue that you need to force.

When working with young people in a drama studio it can sometimes be an effort to get the right work ethic from them. This is partly understandable because there is no performance for an audience. There is no immediate reason to work to get things right. Working hard towards creating theatre is a leap of faith. Working for the camera does not require that leap.

To set out to make a film is very exciting. We would recommend that you aim to do a final take in one shot so that there is no need for editing. Let the camera move to the different areas and try to link those areas by following protagonists. Then let the camera become interested in the new area as the protagonist passes by or joins in.

If you can achieve the one shot, then you can play back the full effect instantly. If you rely on editing, then you are really making a film and the final results will be dictated by the editor. Even if the film ultimately looks better, this might be frustrating for the participants.

chapter six

Devising with words – devising through images

This chapter examines the practical starting points of both words and images as creative stimulants. Drawing on our experience of collaborating with many writers, this chapter also looks at the keys to a successful relationship with a writer in a collaborative environment.

Words as starting points – working physically with text

When working with text you may be setting out on a piece of collaborative new writing or working as choreographer on an existing text. You may even have the title 'movement director' and be asked to consider all physical aspects of the production. We will try to touch on all aspects of creating physicality from words.

For a long time we maintained that the words always came first in our devising process. That rule is not so hard and fast now that we feel more confident about working from images and through physicality. Our experiences on *Stockholm* and *It Snows*, both with Bryony Lavery, have shown us that the physicality can be just as inspiring to the words as the words have proven for the physicality.

When looking for the physical potential within the words, we have to look at those words in several ways. Is there enough space in the text for physicality to flourish? Is there a rich subtext to explore under the words? Do these characters really mean what they say? What do the stage directions offer?

Space

One of our main requirements when commissioning a writer is to consider space. By that we mean the unsaid. This could be rage or sadness or unrequited love. By remaining unsaid they offer rich pickings for choreographed physicality.

Not all of our writers have necessarily delivered this space. That presents us with problems and, shall we say, challenges and opportunities? With some writers the concept of space and the physicality that filled it was central to the writing process. Chris O'Connell's *Hymns*, Abi Morgan's *Tiny Dynamite*, Bryony Lavery's *Stockholm* are all examples of this. We have had to fight for this space on other productions, notably Brendan Cowell's *Rabbit* and Mark Ravenhill's *pool (no water)*. It is important to consider this 'space' when you set out to approach the text physically. Are you empowering the production by having your cast dance across the stage? Are the moves breaking up the rhythm of the show?

We have fallen foul of this on *Stockholm*. We created a physical scene in what we thought was a missing beat from the play. We called it Tea Towels and it charted the mellowing of a couple after an argument. We absolutely loved this tender and complex scene of gradual and grudging reconciliation. Its complexity and simplicity was a bit of an achievement. In isolation it worked well and promised to be a charming crowd pleaser. When we considered it in the production as a whole it was clear that it was destroying the rhythm of Bryony's play and it had to go. It was hard saying good bye to good material but cutting that scene was the most grown up thing either of us have done in our lives. (For those who know us, that will not be such a big surprise.)

For the process behind this scene, see 'Stockholm Fight', page 84.

Subtext

The subtext is crucial. It is very important to aim to express what is not said verbally. If you are reinforcing what has been said verbally, then you are just saying things twice.

The difficult thing to gauge is whether, by articulating the subtext, you are giving the audience something new and valuable or are you just doing their thinking for them? There is little more infuriating and patronising for an audience than to be presented with the latter.

In one of the early drafts of *Hymns*, writer Chris O'Connell was so desperate to give us opportunity for physicality that he set it in the basement of the home of a deceased street performer. The hope was that the numerous props would inspire physicality or, crudely, give us something to do! We had to convince him that his text was full of physical opportunities as it was. It was the characters and what they were saying and, more importantly, not saying to each other that was so rich (see 'Lullaby', page 59).

Hymns was about four men mourning the loss of their friend. It was inspired by the disproportionate number of suicides among young men and how this appeared to be brushed under the carpet. It was about how people do not talk about such things. As this was the case how could we then have our characters, four ordinary men struggling to come to terms with a tragic event, suddenly buck the trend and become eloquent on the matter?

Hymns required a brave writer as all that the words could truthfully express was the characters' inarticulacy and their small talk. It was the physicality and the subtext that had to possess the eloquence. The writer, now fully aware of this, left plenty of space and kept the words bordering on the banal while suggesting this torrent of emotion and questions existing underneath. It became a writer happily writing for the possibilities of a physical approach, allowing images, silence and movement to carry scenes and recognising that, as a writer, he was only part of the theatrical process. (In practice, especially with *Stockholm* and Bryony Lavery, we found that this actually extended the writer's vocabulary rather than limiting it.)

Stage directions

The most obvious area within a text for physicality to flourish is in the stage directions. They are, after all, the bits the writer admits they do not want to express through words. They are, however, a minefield.

On our first production (*Look Back in Anger*) we embraced the stage directions as autocratic demands from the omnipotent author. They were vocalised by the performers and served to highlight how unnatural and uncomfortable they were for characters we wanted to set free. On reflection we were probably just naive, reactionary and trying to make some point that escapes us now. Our adaptation, while aiming to find the original fire at the heart of the play, was less than respectful to the existing text. Stage directions felt like interference and led to a long-standing and unhealthy disregard for them.

It was while working on *Tiny Dynamite* that we developed a new interest in stage directions. Rather than interference, Abi Morgan's stage directions felt like windows through which we could grasp a greater understanding of the world she was creating. This might sound obvious, but what was wonderful about these stage directions was their impossibility. We were instructed to glow in the dark, to climb to the top of an electricity pylon, etc. They were all clips from the film of *Tiny Dynamite* that existed in Abi's head. With the wrong writer this can be a nightmare. Somehow, with Abi, this was a joy – probably because Abi treated the stage directions as windows and opportunities too, rather than demands for prescribed theatricality.

Tiny Dynamite was probably the easiest rehearsal process we have ever experienced. Everyone shared a knowledge and understanding of this film version and everything just fell into place. We knew the world we were aiming for. We knew what it smelled like, tasted like and so on.

Every bizarre stage direction appeared to be linked to an emotion, an effect on the beholder. It was not just about actually being able to climb up the pylon in the middle of an electrical storm. It was the feeling of watching your drunk friend climb up the pylon in the electrical storm. We never spoke about how we were going to literally achieve the pylon and when the scene was presented to Abi, she never questioned its omission because we had captured the essence of the situation – not the construction of metal and wires but the human predicament played out upon it.

Abi also presented us with some unavoidable challenges. She directed the characters to swim about in a lake! We were fearful of being asked to come up with some swimming physicality, but we found a way of solving the issue and, with designer Julian Crouch, decided on how to present the lake. We talked about only ever showing the beginning or end of the swim, the leaping in or scrambling out. The 'lake' became a hole in the decking that constituted the set, under which lay a small plastic paddling pool with an inch of cold (very cold) water in it. We would baste ourselves in the water before surfacing through the hole, dripping wet and exhausted from our 'swim'.

This was one stage direction we were very happy to pass on to someone else. It was also a sign of a true and healthy collaboration that the designer felt he could step in to solve something that could so easily have been someone else's problem.

While working on *Villette* as movement directors we were faced with a script that had **physicalise** written in bold every few pages in what appeared to be a fairly arbitrary fashion. As it turned out, writer Lisa Evans's instinct for what should be a physical scene was pretty sound. Our reticence or reluctance was just a mardy residue of our earlier suspicion of stage directions and their interference in our judgement.

There was a particular stage direction that struck the fear of God into us.

A fire breaks out in the theatre. There is panic.

In what appears now to be a sustained bout of stupidity we feared that what we were being asked to articulate physically was the fire, as it would have been difficult to present through design or lighting. We imagined we were being asked to create an expressive dance piece where people became flames, licking and crackling around the stage!

Once the fear and stupidity passed we realised that it was simply the human predicament that we must articulate. It was the panic and desperation of those trying to escape. It was the strange calm over the face of the one who had given up hope and was resigned to death. It was about strength and weakness. It was about terror and heroism.

There was nothing in the text to map out a story for us other than a fire starts, people try to escape, two central characters rescue a new and important character. This was perfect for us because it gave us everything to create in between the fire and the escape. Here was an example of a stage direction that had terrified us turning out to inspire us. Conversely, there is a stage direction in *Rabbit* by Brendan Cowell that we just could not wait to sink our teeth into: Alone in her parents' holiday home Madeleine wants to seduce her boyfriend, Spin, before her parents turn up. He wants to ingest a cocktail of drugs and then submit to the seduction. Convincing her of the merits of his suggestion she finally relents. Cue stage direction . . .

Kids let loose.

Three perfect words that sum up the situation but also open up a world of debauched possibilities. It suggests Bacchanalian excess and frenzied indulgence. It also captured the social dynamic perfectly. This was a woman in her twenties with her slightly older boyfriend in the prized holiday home of her parents. All of the tension and desire added to the significance of the setting makes them 'kids' again.

Whether Brendan Cowell stumbled upon this phrase in his own rock-and-roll fashion or whether he took hours crafting it does not diminish its genius in our eyes. It was the perfect invitation to play and create. It is that invitation that makes the killer stage direction.

There was also a moment in *Hymns* where the characters flippantly embraced someone's words and turned them into a stage direction. The words 'We could just talk' inspired a camp and expressive torrent of small talk and gestural choreography all based on important subject matters like football, cars, women and DIY.

This scene (see 'Headwrecker', page 61) was more than a dramatic tension release. Set among four friends avoiding the main issues at the funeral of a friend, it also commented on how easy it is to talk. Talking was not the problem. Talking about their feelings and things that mattered appeared to be the

Saskia Butler, *Villette*, 2005

problem. While *Hymns* explored this inability to open up, ultimately it was about our inability to listen when confronted with men speaking about those things that really mattered. The flippancy of Headwrecker set this up well.

Beware the misguided invitation, however! Some stage directions explicitly invite physical creativity, but the task is an empty one and does not move the narrative on. Sometimes they are quite prescriptive and much more like Beckett's stage directions. The author has had all the creativity and just wants you to act them out. We receive many scripts about rock climbing, horse riding, skateboarding, etc. because we are a physical company. This prescriptive physicality is not what we are interested in.

When working with a writer you have the opportunity to discuss such matters. The initial stage directions within *Hymns* were really just to give us opportunities to be busy. We convinced Chris O'Connell that we did not need them as his words were inspiring a physicality that could move the production on and liberate the writing from some of the storytelling.

It is important not to leap at any opportunity to be physical. Like any aspect of a production the physicality must earn its position. Does a physical scene really move things forward? Offering variety to the production is not a good enough reason to leave it in. Let the physicality breathe life into the production by saying something that needs to be said that cannot be said verbally.

How physical is physical?

It is important to remind yourself that you are serving the production as a whole and, in the case of movement direction on an existing play, you are serving that text. Therefore do not get hung up on the spectacular, dynamic or crowd pleasing.

One of our biggest decisions on *Rabbit* was to give the Mother character a tiny moment of stage time on her own. Every word she spoke, every opinion expressed was heinous, but we felt that there must be more to her than this. Here is a woman between a dying husband and a spiteful daughter. We did not want to forgive her obvious deficiencies. We just wanted to present her in three dimensions.

We choreographed a tiny moment when she knew she was alone and allowed the façade to drop for a second. Frightened and unloved by her family, she cradles the live rabbit they have procured for dinner. She holds it tightly. Too tightly. Even this rabbit is going to die and leave her. It was a moment of fear and uncertainty of the future. It made our audience reassess her slightly and by changing the theatrical focus right down to a close-up on her, the unexpected moment of human weakness was as spectacular as any firework.

The questionnaire and devising from a theme

We run workshops throughout the year, all over the country. We also run several residencies at schools and colleges where we take a group, work with them as close to full time as we can get and make an original show with them. These are usually a week long and culminate in a performance at the end of the week. They are very intense periods of creative activity when our devising skills are stretched and tested to the full.

Each residency is different, but one of the consistencies is our use of a specially created questionnaire. We go into each residency with little more than a theme and a few trusted processes to fall back on because we want the show to be about the participants' lives and experiences.

The questionnaire

The questionnaire has been a big part of our creative process. It can be used to inspire both words and physicality. It is a way of opening up worlds unknown and tapping into the experiences of your collaborators. Below is an account of how it came to be used and how we have gone on to use it.

In 1998 Frantic Assembly collaborated with writer Michael Wynne on *Sell Out*. Due to the peculiarities of working with a small-scale touring theatre company, Michael was invited to be part of a project that already had a name, a tour and a poster design before a word had been written. He even had a brief that went along the lines of 'An argument among friends spirals out of control and things can never be the same again'. This was pretty much what we had offered venues to entice them to book the show.

This was the first time we had worked with a recognised writer other than Spencer Hazel and it was a new process for Michael too. Previously we had devised and written together (*Zero*) or worked closely with core collaborator Spencer (*Look Back in Anger, Klub, Flesh*), drawing on our own experiences, ideas and projections. The fear was that Michael could come in and strip that control away from us, although that was also the challenge, and cause for excitement and the reason for engaging this writer in the first place.

Michael's first act was to engage the cast in a series of workshops. One aspect of these workshops was the questionnaire outlined below. The genius of this move was that it invited the cast to offer stories, opinions, details without burdening them with the job of turning that information into a scene. It felt purely a fun exercise with, as you will see, a balance of absurd and probing personal questions. It was also confidential and to this day only he has seen all of our answers.

The brilliance of this approach is that it gathers acres of material, all of which has been collected through what looks like a chaotic questionnaire but is actually a carefully crafted and gently disarming document. It creates a buzz of excitement as the information gets handed back to the writer. It instantly sets up a level of trust between writer and performer and gives the performer an immediate input into the creative writing process.

But this is not play writing by committee. Such a process could have been disastrous and would have been a huge risk considering there was already a tour, a poster, and copy promising certain things to our potential audience. This was still clearly a writer in control. This was his research into the dark possibilities of destructive relationships. The reason for this process was for him to encounter something that would surprise him, to take him into realms he had not considered. It also allowed all the other creatives to have their say in a structured manner and still feel that they were part of that creative process. It asserted order where there could have been chaos.

We have used this process often when devising with young people in residencies. Often these residencies have a broad starting point or theme, e.g. people's experience of their birthdays, or their understanding of loss and death. We all have vastly different experiences and this process allows us all to share or offer our ideas in a safe and confidential way. The revelations from the returned questionnaires are often staggering. We live such varied lives and this gives us an insight into things beyond our imagination. Furthermore, all information is taken as true by the director. It has to be respected. It gives the director an understanding of the life experiences of the people he is working with and, often, making the work for. Invariably the questionnaire responses inspire scenes and text.

When this happens with your questionnaire, the next stage is to talk privately with the person whose questionnaire inspired it. You are about to make the private public and this must be done without dissolving the trust you have recently developed (and need to rely on). You must ask permission to use the information given. It may also be a good idea to encourage the person to lead this scene as it gives them ownership over the idea. Equally you must judge whether it is better, once given permission, to explore the idea maintaining confidentiality.

It is important to construct your questionnaire so that it is full of open questions (i.e. questions that require more than a yes or no answer). You must also find the balance of engaging the participants in a fun and open experience while still creating information that is of use to you. We often start with the questionnaire before telling the participants what the show will be about. This, importantly, keeps their minds open and they don't feel the need to respond in a certain way. The following is Michael's questionnaire for *Sell Out*. It is worth remembering that *Sell Out* was a show that debunked the 'friends are the new family' notion so popular at the time. It was a show full of back-stabbing and sexual shenanigans but, as you can see, the questionnaire seeks to disarm, engage and inspire the participants just as much as it is designed to dig and delve into the scandal of their lives.

The Sell Out Questionnaire

What is your favourite smell? . . . .

Describe a discovery about a friend that shocked you, including your response and that of your pals. . . . .
. . . .
. . . .
. . . .
. . . .
. . . .

What position do you sleep in? . . . .
. . . .
. . . .

List your drunk and drugged regrets. . . . .
. . . .
. . . .
. . . .

What is the worst thing you have stolen? . . . .
. . . .
. . . .

How do you like your eggs? . . . .

Describe something you discovered about a friend that didn't bother you.
. . . .
. . . .
. . . .
. . . .

Describe your best friend's gestures or expressions. . . . .
. . . .
. . . .
. . . .
. . . .
. . . .

Have you ever been drunk on your own – why? . . . .
. . . .
. . . .
. . . .
. . . .
. . . .

Describe a situation where you were misunderstood. . . . .
. . . .
. . . .
. . . .
. . . .

Describe being dumped. . . . .
. . . .
. . . .
. . . .
. . . .

How many Maltesers can you fit in your mouth? . . . .

Have you ever been dumped not face to face? . . . .
. . . .
. . . .

Mobile phones – discuss. . . . .
. . . .
. . . .
. . . .
. . . .
. . . .

What have you done that was illegal? . . . .
. . . .
. . . .
. . . .

What were you really into when you were young that you now really hate?
. . . .
. . . .
. . . .
. . . .

Is there anything you wanted to do when you were young but not now – what
changed? . . . .
. . . .
. . . .
. . . .
. . . .

Describe an argument that made you storm off. . . . .
. . . .
. . . .
. . . .
. . . .

Faxes – discuss. . . . .
. . . .
. . . .
. . . .
. . . .

Ever been caught slagging someone off? . . . .
. . . .
. . . .
. . . .

What have you bought that you really didn't need? . . . .
. . . .
. . . .
. . . .

If depressed, what cheers you up? . . . .
. . . .
. . . .

Internet/E-mail – discuss. . . . .
. . . .
. . . .
. . . .
. . . .

Have you ever insulted or offended someone and regretted it? . . . .
. . . .
. . . .
. . . .

What do you want most in the world? . . . .
. . . .
. . . .

What are our generation's specific problems? . . . .
. . . .
. . . .
. . . .
. . . .
. . . .

What makes you get out of bed? . . . .
. . . .

Did video kill the radio star? . . . .
. . . .

Samuel James and Georgina Lamb fight in the kitchen in *Stockholm*, 2007

Keir Charles looks for moral support from Mark Rice-Oxley, Cait Davis and Leah Muller in *pool (no water)* by Mark Ravenhill, 2006 © Manuel Harlan

Karl Sullivan, Joseph Traynor, Steven Hoggett and Eddie Kay share some home truths in *Hymns*, 2005

Samuel James and
Georgina Lamb enjoy the last dance in
Stockholm, 2007 © Manuel Harlan

Scott tries to work it all out in *Heavenly*, 2004 (Brits off Broadway)

Paul Anderson
in *Market Boy*, 2006

Imogen Knight in *Dirty Wonderland*, 2005

Jimmy Akingbola (Othello) observing Claire-Louise Cordwell (Desdemona) in *Othello*, 2008 © Manuel Harlan

The residencies

Residencies are just as intensive for us as they are for the participants. We aim for a slick and dynamic show for a paying public in four days. These pressured creative sessions often serve as opportunities to try out ideas we might want to take forward into our own productions.

The questionnaire is a crucial part of disarming and engaging the participants of the many creative residencies we lead at schools and colleges around the country. For each residency we choose a theme we want to explore and then ask the participants about their thoughts and experiences on the theme. Just as above, the answers to these questions inspire both words and physical scenes.

Below are the questionnaires we used on specific residencies. We hope that they might illuminate our initial creative processes, but hopefully they will also serve to show how simple the primary idea behind each project was.

Dreamscape

With Dreamscape we wanted to explore people's dreams. This ranges from the random images flitting through the brain while asleep to their long-term aspirations. This is a very rich and fertile territory to explore with young people. The questionnaire set out to get a whole range of answers, light and dark.

Dreamscape Questionnaire

Do you dream in colour or black and white?
Do you have a recurring dream?
Do you have a recurring nightmare?
Did/Do you keep anything under your bed?
If you daydream, where do you put yourself?
Have you ever dreamt you were with somebody famous?
Have you ever dreamt an event before it actually happened?
Have you ever dreamt an ability for yourself?
Have you ever woken up crying and why?
Have you ever woken up laughing and why?
List any dream analysis you know.
Has anyone dreamt of you – what were you like or what did you do?
Does anyone recur in your dreams?
Do you have a pre-bed routine?
Do you take your clothes off in a certain order before bed?

How many toilet trips do you make in one night?

Do you have any particular sleeping habits – sleepwalking or sleep talking, etc.?

Class

Class was about the participants' experiences of school and the people around them. The questionnaire is probably a little more focused (a little too focused?) on the subject matter. This can give limited results.

Class Questionnaire

Who is/was your favourite teacher and why?

Who is/was your worst teacher and why?

List the things you used to do in the playground.

Describe your happiest school day.

Describe your worst school day.

What was your best and favourite subject?

What was your worst and least favourite subject?

Are qualifications important and why?

How many of your class friends now are for life?

Have you ever had detention and why?

Have you ever been given lines – why and what were they?

Describe your most frightening moment in class.

Have you ever been treated unfairly?

What do teachers do at the weekend?

Was your first kiss at school and if so, where?

Have you ever had a crush on a teacher or classmate?

Have you ever told a big lie at school – what was it?

What would you teach?

What would you turn into a subject for study at school?

Bedism

Everyone spends a lot of their life in their bed. Bedism looked to explore the different beds we experience from our cots to our death beds.

Bedism Questionnaire

Have you ever had monsters under your bed? Describe them.

Describe your first bed.

Describe the last time you cried in bed.
Describe the last time you laughed in bed.
Who is your dream bed partner?
Who is your nightmare bed partner?
What is the largest number of people you have shared a bed with?
What stories, if any, were you told in bed?
What keeps you awake at night?
What kept you awake at night when you were younger?
What were you sent to bed for?
Do you eat in bed? What?
How many sexual partners do you think you'll have?
Have you ever seen a dead body?
Have you ever faked illness?
What is the strangest experience you have had in a bed?
What position do you sleep in?

Scar Tissue

Scar Tissue was about how we get hurt and how we recover. We wanted to find out all the ways in which the participants had been hurt and how they felt about that.

Scar Tissue Questionnaire

Who do you regret hurting?
Tell us about your best day ever.
Tell us about your worst day ever.
Who would you say sorry to but never did? Why?
What is the worst present you have ever received?
What is your best physical feature?
What is your worst physical feature?
What is your most hated food?
What do you WANT to be when you are 30?
What WILL you be when you are 30?
Have you ever been in an accident? Describe it.
Have you ever been dumped not face to face?
What was your most humiliating moment?
What last made you laugh?
How many stitches do you have? Where? Why?
Have you ever been stood up?

You can see how we try to winkle stories out of people through the questionnaire. Other residency titles/themes included:

Terminus

This residency was all about being dumped or dumping someone. It is an experience most people have been part of and personal accounts can range from the comic to the tragic.

Protection

Admitting your love and recognising those you will fight to the death over was at the heart of our Protection residency. It explored how you would feel if they were kept or taken from you.

Gift

Everyone has a birthday. Our experiences of them will vary greatly. How will the birthdays of our past compare to the birthdays of our future? Where and what will you be? And who will you be with?

Deliverance

We receive letters throughout our life. From birthday cards to letters of love to exam results to bills to letters of condolence, they all come through our letterbox. What are you wanting to come through the letterbox? What would be the best delivery ever? What would you write down and place through someone else's letterbox?

The 'It Snows' model

We have occasionally set out with a writer to create work that is image based. This may seem contradictory but we were looking to employ the writer's sensibility concerning storytelling and dramatic arc. Within the creative team they have a unique perspective and a valuable input into this essentially physical and visual process.

An added bonus is that the process might inspire words.

What follows is the outcome of a couple of days' research and development between ourselves, Bryony Lavery and a few trusted performers. We were testing ideas and searching for inspiration for our *It Snows* project for the National Theatre Connections 2008. We were one of ten commissioned projects where a writer (in this case three writers – Bryony Lavery, Scott Graham and Steven Hoggett) creates a play to be performed by young companies thoughout the country. Our project was a brave new step in that it set out to instruct and inspire a company through a physical production.

We entered the rehearsal room with our simple but evocative/instructive title *It Snows*, various DVDs and photographs, and a load of CDs. We played and set up various tasks and improvisations. We talked about our experiences of snow and quickly the world of *It Snows* started to open up, offering us more than enough material for our play.

The following, it is hoped, will show you how such simple themes can open out into rich and complex worlds. Occasionally you will find names mentioned, e.g. Eddie or Delphine. These were the names of the practitioners involved in the process. The text below is taken from the collated session notes from the research and development at the National Theatre Studio. They show how ideas became skeletal sketches and how they, in turn, came to life.

Some initial starting points – ideas and images

Things left behind that don't make sense any more – (The snowman) the stones, the scarf, the carrot.

Frozen clothes on a washing line, caught mid-dance.

Old people set against the elements, struggling against the blizzard.

First steps in virgin snow – who has ownership? The perfection – the desire to preserve the pristine.

Dressing for the elements – multiple clothes – invincible feeling.

Everything sounds different.

Snow under urban sodium light.

Snow for the elderly or frail.

Blood on snow – Eddie's story of 'Xmas coming up the path' – his uncle and aunty approaching in the snow, full of festivity, when she falls and smashes her mouth on the floor. Blood everywhere.

Snow and extreme cold – fun for a minute and then not fun. Dangerous. Mortal danger.

The person left behind – behind the curtains watching others in the snow. Fear of snow or attack.

The child's desire to experience the snow and the adult's need to revisit it.

Some characters (building on the initial thoughts)

Old couple fighting the elements. Seen as heroic? Tragic? Fearful of the snow? They also possess the potential for liberation and nostalgia and romance. They could embrace the snow, fall into it and lie still. Then they suddenly start giggling and making snow angels. Or are they the couple who Eddie and Vicki created? Is he dressing her up to go out? Is he going out too? If not, is this an act of cruelty? Of euthanasia? Is he turning her into Capt. Oates from the Scott expedition? Does he put a letter in her pocket and send her off? Paddington style? And what would the note say? 'Please look after this lady'. Is it him who is about to die/commit suicide and the only way to save her is to set her out into the snow? No-one comes calling to the house so she would just sit there with the body. He is protecting her from that?

The woman behind the net curtain. Why won't she come out? And why does she watch the others? If she did not like the snow, would she be so obsessed with the others playing in it? Does she want to be invited out? Does she just need the safety net and reassurance?

The new parent who cannot wait to share the joy of snow. But all the child can feel is fear and uncertainty. This is not what he thought parenting was about. He has to fight the idea that the child has in some way let him down.

Heroic Yorkshire dads. Every year they start the ritual of building the biggest snowman for miles around. They start on one street and take in another three on their route. All the kids follow, as do the wives in a mutual reinforcement of gender stereotypes. But this is all about pride in those stereotypes. The snow gets cleared from the streets. Cars, kids and pets are missing, all consumed by the epic snowman.

The policeman stuck in his car in a ditch. He is incapacitated by this. He is useless. There is nothing he can do. And once the fear and panic and sense of duty subside he is enormously and joyously liberated.

ASBO boys. Menacing and utterly joyous. Under a sullen street lamp they skulk and loiter, but as the flakes descend they become Gene Kelly singing in the snow. But only when they feel that we can't see them and they can't see us.

The evil snowball maker, packing the most perfectly destructive snowball of this or any other lunchtime. As the playground gradually cottons on to him an exclusion zone develops. He is oblivious.

The family whose car has the last piece of snow on it. Where have they come from? How have they maintained this? Are they actually trying to keep it on?

The 'beachcombing' path clearer finding things lost to the snow. Clues (in his head?) to great mysteries?

The accidental lovers whose affair can only last as long as the snow.

The observers of the snowball fight.

More detailed ideas – some physical

1   Car. Trapped in the snow? Child in the back watching an argument in front. An apology is inspired/forced by the child. She unclips her belt and puts mum's and dad's hands together.

    Is the parents' behaviour shaped or modified by the trapped situation and the presence of the child?

    During the argument the child has been collecting snow. She chooses her moment to release the tension and her snowball. It is the last thing anyone expects inside the car. Do they break out of the car to continue the snow fight? Do they sit there shamed by this protest, snow melting in their hair? Who will apologise/speak first?

    Does she write her protest/situation on the steamed up windows? Do the parents note this and turn to their own windows and scribe their own predicament and feelings?

2   The romantic snowman. A prankster sets about making a little snowman appear on someone's front doorstep. They somehow smooth the snow on their exit and ring the bell. The person opens the door to find the little snowman looking up at them with no explanation as to how it got there and who was responsible. It is obvious that the snowman just wants to come in (or wants you to come out).

Does the snowman have a flower in his hand? Or an item of significance? Found by the beachcomber?

3   Milkman, postman and paperboy meet at same time at house. The snow in front of the house is pristine. Who steps in the snow first? How can they minimise damage? Can they only leave one set of footprints? (PHYSICAL)

4   Another prankster creating another mystery. Two of them, each manipulating a giant shoe. The world wakes to find a giant has walked among them.

5   The sliding car. Delphine and her dad. The wheels lock on the car and it skids inexorably towards the bumper of another car. Time slows down. She looks at him. How will he react to the impending situation. Is this a time to talk? To kiss? How far can we stretch this moment?

6   The chaos of the playground. Or the large group of friends? Or the whole school liberated and bursting out into the snow field. Charlie Brown/Bash Street Kids physicality – a cloud of limbs, joyous and exhilarating – punctuated by the sudden structure of the snowflake. A celebration of its form. Groups of six fleetingly swap chaos for crystalline structure before returning to chaos. A Busby Barclay meets Tom Brown's School Days number. (PHYSICAL)

7   Keeping warm. A couple look after each other, making sure that nothing of their loved one is exposed and at risk. Tender and sensual choreography belonging to lovers. (PHYSICAL)

8   The simple physicality and joy of catching snowflakes. (PHYSICAL)

9   First steps. Pristine snow. A palette to paint on. Patterns in the snow. Inventive. A game. A challenge. (Fleetingly told horizontally if possible? Using a back wall as a floor so we see the footsteps from above?) This is Banksy in the snow. (PHYSICAL)

10 Snow angels. Art again. This time with the possibility of cuddle and caress. It may start as two but can open out. We see them join larger groups. They are all together. They all occasionally get up to look at their work. (PHYSICAL)

11 A list of ten things you can't do wearing mittens.

12   *The snowball fight.*

Shirley and Denise. Hard on the outside, fragile inside. They are the cool girls. But they are a bit rubbish. They will date really badly. Being hit by a snowball is the death of cool. They are here to gawp at Darren.

The tough ones. Boy and girl. She is acting tough but is quickly out of her depth. The bad boys are hitting back. Boy and girl are both obliterated by snowballs.

The blossoming lovers. Maybe they have not even acknowledged the affection they are beginning to share. As they watch the snowball fight they feel they could be in a film – Love Story without the cancer. When the fight starts to spill over they are desperate not to let the fragile developing bond between them be trashed. Even when she takes a good one full in the face she still manages to smile through gritty snow and bleeding gums. Desperate not to lose the moment, they persevere, even when he takes one in the knackers and then another to the neck. Eventually they can remain in denial no longer. They, and their young love, are targets of a thoughtless and cruel mob.

13   *Businessmen stand on a station platform as the snow falls. Gradually they begin to huddle for warmth. They have take-away coffee cups in one hand, their briefcases in another. They put the case on their feet, protecting it from the ground. Then the coffee cup goes over their nose and, tightly huddled, they become a heroic penguin community battling the elements and protecting what is dear to them. (Is this a final image? Do we see the businessmen throughout, forever waiting?)*

14   *Bin men in the snow. Picking up black bags and setting themselves against the elements like Arctic explorers. The bags are full of polystyrene balls. The bags have holes in them. Throwing them around releases the 'snow' (with a little help from a wind machine?). Again it is the dynamic of the adult reliving what is lost. Liberated from being an adult. Maybe this happens every morning and you would witness it if you rose silently with the dawn chorus. Maybe the birds sing to the dustmen and the milkmen when no-one is looking. It is their secret.*

1   We set the performers the task of creating more stories specifically considering SCENARIO, RELATIONSHIP, and PHYSICALITY (all set indoors).

   a)   Waiting for a lift. ***Black Out. Lights Up.***

   b)   The couple who are going nowhere and are quite happy. Coiled and curled around each other they delicately groom one another.

   c)   A similar couple trapped but going mad. One picks fluff off the other. The other watches them. They then pick fluff off their partner. The partner takes the fluff and puts it back. ***Black Out.***

      Lights Up. They again pick fluff off. This time one of them accidentally(?) rips the other's shirt. ***Black Out.***

      Lights Up. They are both sitting there quite calmly with their clothes in tatters. ***Black Out.***

   d)   Dressing someone who is incapable. Preparing them for the cold. But only one of them is getting dressed. Why? (See old couple fighting the elements.) Is this comic? Is it all in vain because they cannot open the door? Is it euthanasia we are witnessing?

2   The dramatic arc of snow.

One of our most important discoveries was what we called the dramatic arc of snow. This became a major influence on the structure of It Snows.

   a)   Expectation or anticipation. It might snow

   b)   It is snowing

   c)   Snow is here. It has landed

   d)   It is tainted. Dirty. Melting

   e)   It is gone.

What does the snow cover? What does it bring? What does it reveal when it has gone?

We split the team up into groups of three and asked them to construct stories using the structure of this dramatic arc. An example of one of the results is set out below:

a)   They have found her mother

b)   She walks into a room full of people who could be her mother

c)   One stands up. This is her mother

d)   It becomes clear that the mother does not want to be there

e)   There is no connection. They have to part.

The stories were simple frameworks and dramatic arcs upon which you could build much more complex stories.

· · ·

Not everything made it into the final draft of *It Snows*. In the end we were quite sparse with the suggested imagery *because* we had had such a good time and were so successful thinking up possibilities. We decided to leave enough room for the people performing *It Snows* to come up with their own images and explore their own experiences.

Stockholm day one and the *Stockholm* recipe

People are often intrigued by what we take into the first days of rehearsal and what we get from a research and development session. The process is different for each show, but we thought it might be interesting to focus on the development of *Stockholm* (written by Bryony Lavery), specifically the notes from the first and last days of the session.

This development session took place over two weeks in December 2007 at the National Theatre Studio in London.

Bodies present in the room were Scott Graham, Steven Hoggett, Bryony Lavery, Daniel Evans, Mandy Lawrence, Delphine Gaborit, Ben Wright and Lyndsey Turner.

Below are the notes and points of discussion for the first day.

As is clear, the discussions were broad and at times fairly random. We didn't set any particular end point or agenda on the day. Instead, it serves as a record of the free association we like to encourage in the room and how such diverse thoughts and references have an uncanny way of constructing a kind of intellectual parameter, an outer limit that inversely begins to define the space in which the eventual show might begin to form itself. Where a book title is referenced, it might have been that someone simply asked whether anyone had read it. On some occasions this might have been followed by a discussion of the central issues it covered, but this was not always the case. One of the most controversial joys of the modern intellectual age is the capacity to 'believe' something to be the case without having actually experienced it. Dangerous but in some instances quite handy. We know for a fact that some people in the room talked about the Brian Keenan book as if they had read it from cover to cover when we now know this was not actually true. Not that this got in the way of some healthy discourse you understand. In the case of quotations, we rarely make a note of who said what. This might be to protect the person or might be an act of abject laziness. It's most probably a bit of both.

Brian Keenan book An Evil Cradling.

Patty Hearst.

A Carol Churchill text presenting a list of atrocities as 'a love story'.

John Fowles book The Collector.

Manipulative uses of language.

Question – does power shift as soon as one person commits a physically violent act?

'I was there to be smacked for something that had happened years before.'

Lolita and the idea that the man is not to blame at the critical moment.

'To whack someone is really a strategy to have your needs met.'

Could loving [physical] material lead to fighting?

Could fighting [physical] material lead to loving?

The Cornelia Parker effect – how a lunch box, a laundry basket and a coat hanger, once inanimate objects, become deadly weapons.

Film – What's Love Got to Do with It – scene in the car where Ike and Tina fight then are forced to step out of a limousine into a high-profile event with blood on their clothing.

'Close the fucking door' – is it more aggressive when loud or quiet?

Audience – to give them a sense of observation, of involved responsibility, of being questioned.

Control = a little girl with dolls.

Cushioning – making things seem quieter, more stable.

'If you fall in love when you are young, you can always remember them as something else. This else-ness is very important in understanding why they are together.'

Film – Code Unknown.

Film – The Piano Teacher.

The idea of physical proficiency as a signifier for shared history together – they move beautifully together – sex, the washing up, shopping away.

Songs and singing – why do you sing? What do you sing? Singing to yourself or to them?

Music – why do you put it on? To appease, annoy, dupe, unsettle, cover up?

The sound of meat slapping on a table.

Music – the characters are hearing it and are in control.

Appetite – knives and forks dance. Eating each other.

Film – 9 Songs.

Music – album plays constantly. Music as apt commentary. Incongruous music.

Periods of prolonged silence.

Taking loved music off so it's not tainted by a bad experience.

Asking about the best sex ever had, not just between them.

Dali painting – Autumnal Cannibalism.

Beautiful South record cover for We Are Each Other.

Not being able to commit to the argument because the football scores are on so even the argument is rubbish.

Question – when does 'I' become 'you' when telling of an event?

Arguments – where and how do they happen? Hanging a painting, map reading, moving furniture, wrapping presents (being reduced to the function of a finger pressed for sticky tape).

Physical Exercise (A practical exercise):

Pull partner in to yourself so there is no space between you. Give full support. Take the weight. Little lifts. Take them to the floor.
One pair on the floor, one pair on the table.

· · ·

The list above shows the range of discussion on just day one. Over the next few days we explored all aspects of a loving but destructive relationship and the associated themes of Stockholm syndrome.

On the last day of the development we devised what we called a recipe. We felt that these were all the ingredients that had come out of the development and should go into the further development of the text, of the story. We had unearthed a vast amount of information and ideas in the preceding days. We tried to distil them into the simplest form to provide a framework, a skeletal structure we could then flesh out. The recipe is also set out as a dramatic arc:

A couple
Us
A day
Some events
A plea. Some demands. (An ultimatum – the deadline is reached and passed)
A recipe/A confession

A meal is cooked
The last dance
(The end of the world)

It might be really useful to think about your development work progressing in this way. Of course, you should not necessarily be reductive, but devised theatre and the nature of devising theatre can often mean that we take our focus off things like the dramatic arc.

The final production was remarkably faithful to the recipe above. The recipe served to consolidate all of the input from a sprawling development session and then take us forward in a structured fashion.

(It should be pointed out that the development session was sprawling only in the amount of good work that needed to be processed, not in the amount of time we had to indulge. We are very careful about this. We even stopped the *Stockholm* sessions two days early because we felt that we had created enough. We believe you have to look out for the point where research and development or even rehearsal stops being productive and stop it there. Otherwise you taint the whole thing.)

Actions speak louder than words?

Sometimes they do. It is also good to remember that sometimes actions fall completely flat, can seem obscure, strange, pretentious, needless, pointless, clichéd, simplistic, indulgent . . . (the list goes on).

Movement has to earn its place in any production. Even for a 'physical theatre' company we have to be sure that the decision to create a movement scene is based on it being the best way of telling the story. No writer worth their salt wants a production to merely dance all over their words. Movement has to fight for its existence at every turn.

When thinking about movement versus words we often consider distillation. How can the crux of the matter be distilled and presented most effectively?

If that choice is to present something physically, then we have to ask ourselves whether we have created a three-minute movement scene to put across what it would have taken three seconds to say verbally. If so, then you may be saying the same thing for three minutes if the meaning is obvious in the movement, or it may be that the movement is so obscure that it takes a full three minutes for the audience to get something they could have got in three seconds. Either way does not make for a happy audience or good theatre.

We would encourage you to think about this distillation. An example of this kind of thought is the Happy Hour scene from *Dirty Wonderland*.

The basic premise was that the central character, Alex, lost his girlfriend in the sprawling hotel as soon as they checked in for their dirty weekend. He is told that she is down in the bar. It is happy hour. He sets off to find her but only encounters a couple trying to relive their honeymoon but failing miserably. There is a suggestion that he might be seeing a future version of him and his girlfriend. What is clear is that the fire in this other relationship has gone out no matter how hard they try to go through the moves.

We wanted the audience to know that the couple really are making an effort and that there was a time when they really would have set the room alight with their love. Now that this has faded they are left with little more than routine and mutual contempt.

We believed in this rich scenario – even more so when one of the cast found out that his parents actually did have their honeymoon in the hotel we were performing in and even returned years later to find that it had lost its magic! This seemed to validate the scenario. (The resulting scene cast no aspersions over the strength of the performer's parents' marriage!)

We talked about how we could get the history of these people across to our audience and how this history comes crashing to the ground in the present moment. It became a complex thing to solve through text. There seemed to be an unavoidable need for dull exposition. There appeared to be more merit in their sudden physicality expressing the exposition. Instantly this was about love and passion. Just as instantly we could see it fade and be replaced by bitterness.

The scene played out as follows:

The couple sit side by side as a singer appears to croon forlornly. They, apart from Alex, are the only people in the bar. The man gets up and gestures, ordering a couple of drinks. The two of them sit together again. Suddenly they burst into a passionate and provocative dance. It is full of daring and danger. Just as suddenly their dance ends. They are sat again. Their drinks arrive. The waiter places a gin and tonic in front of the lady and a pint of lager in front of the man. When the waiter leaves, the man reaches for the gin and the woman reaches for the pint.

Just when you think this is the joke, they both casually spit into the drinks they hold and place them back in front of their partner. Then, seemingly oblivious or knowing but past caring, they both drink from the drinks in front of them. This moment is a shocking acceptance of the contempt from their partner. It may even be an acceptance of guilt for letting the spark die.

This became so much more complex (and pleasing) than we could have hoped for if we had opted for words. The moment and the physicality had been distilled into a single action (the spit). The exposition was the passionate precursor to this act.

(Think about the ending of Brokeback Mountain. *The beautiful economy of the shirt inside the shirt, reversing the way they were kept before, and the* simple, enigmatic 'Jack, I swear . . .' Perfect distillation of words and action. God bless Ang Lee! See 'Working with writers', below.)

If it is not about distillation then, alternatively, aim for progression through your choice of physicality. Demand that it moves the story on! Consider what words cannot do or can only do in an obvious or laboured way. In *Hymns* we chose movement and clichéd jokes to suggest frustration and verbal inarticulacy. The characters' discomfort grew and exploded as they skirted verbally around the real issues that concerned them. It would have been wrong in the context of *Hymns* to have the four men eloquently express their pain and fear of words through text. That pushed us towards movement as, in this context, actions would definitely speak louder than words.

Simply, we would like to think we don't just throw shapes because we can. There are many tools at your disposal as a theatre maker. It is crucial to use the right one at the right time.

Working with writers

Your practical relationship with writers is as idiosyncratic as the writers themselves and the project you are working on. We have not committed to any one process because every time we think we might have found one something comes along to blow that out of the water. Any single and constant process would surely be reductive or claustrophobic anyway?

This is the most important relationship to have clear and understood from the start. You both must know what you expect of each other. Sometimes you can only find this by getting together and trying things rather than talking about it, as from the outside we can all have a slightly different understanding of ourselves and how we actually are under pressure. Any research and development session you can find the time and money for could be crucial to this understanding. You need to know where your creative references are. You need to know whether the writer is expected/willing/able to write in the rehearsal room. You need to know if your writer is going to take inspiration from the devising processes or whether they need the privacy to follow their own clear line of creativity and then pass that on to you/the devising company.

This is not something we have always got right. It is from bitter and exhausting experience that we stress the importance of this relationship.

Acknowledging the range of possibilities here, we will not try to advocate a single process. Instead, what follows is taken from a workshop we held for writers looking to gain an understanding of how to incorporate physicality into their work. Or how to bring the inherent physicality out. The rest of this section sees a slight change in focus as we address the writers themselves.

This workshop dealt with the writer's desire to bring physicality to their work. It hopefully showed how to write with this in mind while always leaving space for the input of other collaborators. Areas we wanted the writer participants to consider were:

1 Inspiration for words
2 Harnessing physicality
3 Helping others to harness physicality
4 Space and economy
5 Other worlds and ingredients (music, songs, lighting, etc.).

The writers were shown four images and asked for their first responses. This basically explores the cliché/truth that an image speaks a thousand words. The images were promotional images of Frantic Assembly, but they could be any reportage photography, or even the work of photographers like Gregory Crewdson. In their responses, the writers talked in depth about the stories behind the images. There was not necessarily agreement but there was always emotional depth.

The writers were then shown an edited promotional film of *pool (no water)*. None of the participants had seen the show yet. This film has roughly chronological images but no sound. Instead there is the track 'The Moment I Said It' from the album *Speak For Yourself* by Imogen Heap laid on top.

Again they were asked to give their reactions. It was remarkable how much of the story they had got just from the edited images. More intriguingly they had a very strong sense of all the emotional relationships that existed in the real show. It was then pointed out to the writers that they had been manipulated by the ingredients of the film – the selection of music, the editing, the choice of focus, the colours, as well as the performances.

The exercise served to show the economy with which you can manipulate emotion and tell a story. And all without a single word. This was not to make the writer redundant. This was to inspire the writer to think about writing in a different way.

Bedworld

We used a couple of volunteers to be the couple in the Stockholm Bed task (see page 160). We ran the exercise and then noted the complex and fragile stories that emerged. The writers were then asked to state the instructions for the task as succinctly as possible while capturing something of the essence of the world the performers create.

It was agreed that these short sentences could effectively be the stage directions for the Bedworld task. (It was pointed out that this was how the stage directions in *Stockholm* emerged.) If those words could sum up the instructions, could the same words then work in reverse and inspire the delicacy and sensitivity of the Stockholm Bed task? This example showed the writers how stage directions could be incredibly simple and inspiring if they have an idea of the world they wish to explore. Imagining that world should draw upon their freedom of imagination. It should not be bogged down by thinking about the technicality of the resulting choreography. Leave that to the particular skills of the performers/choreographer/director. That is why they are in the room.

We talked about stage directions at length, using our chequered history of being on the receiving end of them to illustrate examples of good and bad practice (see 'Words as starting points – working physically with text', page 169).

Writers can be just as guilty as performers and directors of giving their audience too much. To illustrate this we followed Stockholm Bed with the Leg of Lamb exercise (see page 214), showing that a whole new story can emerge through the most minute change in dynamic within text. (The change of tense again prompted the story of a woman confessing to having killed and cooked her husband!) This led to us discussing economy within writing.

Economy

We considered things that were greater than the sum of their parts. We played a few songs including 'Wichita Lineman', written by Jimmy Webb and performed by Glen Campbell. This song is a masterclass in suggesting depth and troubled human emotions. It presents a telecommunications worker fixing lines beside the road. He is tired and missing a loved one but is compelled by a sense of duty and concern for the job in hand to keep working rather than take a holiday. If you were to look at the words, this is all they convey.

But this song has the power to bring tears to a glass eye! Surely there is more to it than this? We then considered the ingredients:

- *The words*: There is a tension in the scenario between the duty to the job and the implications for many people if the job is not done properly versus the tiredness and love and longing for another person.
- *The delivery of the words*: Glen Campbell imbues the words with a considerable weight. This is not a fleeting thought during a lunch break.

- *The music*: The bass is heavy and mournful. The strings are highly emotive. The general tone is sad. We are not music experts. These were the comments and observations from the listeners.

All of this appeared to overwhelmingly suggest that we were listening to some epic story of distant love and misguided duty. All in 3 minutes and 7 seconds, the last 37 seconds of which was just slowly fading music; and in just 15 lines of text, 3 of which are a repeat.

It has an incredible economy. We looked at the writing specifically and noted that we had all projected a greater meaning onto what appeared to be there. How had this happened? And what had we projected onto the song? What had we brought to the experience of listening to the song?

The text presents a very succinct tension.

The sound of the loved one is crashing into the Lineman's mundane work. He is not taking time out to think about this love. It is forcing its way into his head. He is trying to focus on the work despite this voice calling him back. Remember, the Wichita Lineman is *still* on the line.

The tension within these lines gets carried through the rest of the song so that lines about needing a holiday but being worried about his workload begin to express a tragic human frailty, the dangers of a life unlived, economic pressures on the working man, time passing by, and the utterly heroic act of a man putting the effectiveness of a phone network above his own heart and body!

By the time we had got to the killer lines about needing more than wanting and wanting for all time we were all virtually in tears!

This song is epic. It is minute. At times our projection of backstory can seem absurd, but this is what we bring to things with this kind of economy and power to suggest and engage. We, as listeners, have done most of the work in telling this story.

Is this accidental? Jimmy Webb has said that 'Wichita Lineman' was written as a response to a challenge where he said he could write a song about anything and then saw a lineman at work. It could not be simpler. There is nothing accidental about the tone of the music or the delivery of the lyrics. They are surely working to engage us in seeing the Lineman's life in a certain way without being explicit about it.

It was clear that the complete song is successful because of the way the ingredients had been considered and played off one another and with each other to suggest so much more than they explicitly say. This is why it is so successful and affecting for the listener.

There are many lessons to be learnt here, not just from the economy of song writing but also through this use of ingredients. All composers and lyricists write songs to be sung. Writers need to remember that they are writing plays to be performed and should give full consideration to the potential ingredients involved.

Writing Silence

Writing Silence was another task designed to get the writers to think about writing in a different way.

We played the end of *The Ice Storm*, the film directed by Ang Lee (making sure that those who did not want to know the score looked away). The scene (again, look away if you do not want to know the final score) involves Tobey Maguire's character returning home on a train after it has become trapped by an ice storm. He is obviously pleased and surprised to see his family pick him up from the station. He does not comment on the fact that his younger brother is not with them (he has been killed in a freak accident the night before; Tobey Maguire does not know this). When the family get in the car, the atmosphere changes and it falls to father Kevin Kline to break the news to his son. He turns to look at him in the backseat and his son smiles back obliviously. This is too much for the father and he breaks down crying. The mother caresses her husband's back and tears well in the eyes of the young sister. Slowly there is a terrible dawning across the face of Tobey Maguire. The film ends without anything else being said.

Again this is a brilliantly brave example of craftsmanship and economy from Ang Lee and his creative team and performers. It is a very brave scene as it never gives us what we think we are waiting for – namely, an answer to the question 'how is he going to break the news?' Instead it gives us something much more human, complex, engaging and ultimately more rewarding.

The first impression was that this near-silent scene had been shown as an example of what writers cannot write. It was actually meant to display the opposite. This being film, every aspect of this scene would have been written to allow for the correct positioning of cameras and lighting. There would have been a very clear script for people to follow.

We were not suggesting that writers dictate the angle of a performer's face or the lighting design. We were suggesting they take inspiration from the complexity and precision of scenes that were written to be silent. We wanted to stress that a writer can write their ideas in images when it is apt to do so.

The poignancy of inarticulacy

We are fed up of people on stage suddenly expressing their inner woes in the most eloquent fashion. Taking the notion of how powerful theatre can be when the audience engages and completes the narrative, we have dabbled with another aspect of union between economy and projection. For the sake of sounding clever and considered we will call it 'The poignancy of inarticulacy'.

The writers' workshop touched on this and talked about the dangers and pitfalls associated with it. We talked about how our production *Hymns* faced the dilemma of how a bunch of inarticulate men could express themselves truthfully yet still convey the complexity of their emotion when the whole show was about the difficulty of doing so. We spoke of how it quickly became clear that the words might not be the right or apt medium for expressing this complex dilemma (see 'Lullaby', page 59).

Again here we were talking about how we might get words to suggest more than they appear to at face value. We then played another song where the writer seemed to have given up on the attempt at articulacy but had instead given a moving poignancy to that inarticulacy (and in doing so inspired us to give it this title).

The song was 'My Blue Wave' by Lambchop, from the album *Is a Woman*, specifically the fourth verse from 'And William called. . .' to 'Sometimes, William, we're just screwed'.

The lyrics perfectly illustrate a situation where words could not help or at least where the character was unable to use the correct words (even William 'tried to tell' about his sister's boyfriend). Nobody is able to use words. The situation itself is so specific (not knowing what to say to someone who is calling because he does not know what to say to a sister whose boyfriend has just died) that there appears to be no manual for dealing with it. What we are left with is the suggestion of pain and the inability to help. The central character cannot help William, who cannot help his sister.

It is within the gaps left unresolved that the humanity of this song lies. It is not that they do not want to help; it is just that the lack of articulacy, pain and suffering are parts of life, as are the love and concern that compelled William to make the call for help. It is the lack of words said that leaves this situation open and interesting. Even the conclusion, 'Sometimes, William, we're just screwed', does not suggest finality. It leaves us with the impression of people left to struggle on.

We talked about how the key to writing with this kind of economy might be about harnessing a human predicament and then it is this that engages the audience and makes them wilfully work so hard. 'Wichita Lineman', *The Ice Storm* and 'My Blue Wave' all articulate very human predicaments but none of them aim for textual eloquence. The eloquence somehow seems to exist in the spaces around the words. The lesson was that this is never an accident and for each example there is a writer embracing the ingredients they can lay their hands on and crafting their work with economy and precision.

chapter seven

Textual analysis

GETTING SCENES ON THEIR FEET

In this chapter we present some simple exercises to encourage practitioners to see text from a basic physical viewpoint and from there attach the discoveries back to the text.

The Lecture

We make no apologies for the simplicity of this exercise. Sometimes it is important to address the basics.

Recently we have been working with actors on Shakespearian text and it has been startling to see how many actors retreat behind an adopted tone of voice, a faux classical RP. They then crash on with a jaunty rhythm in the hope that the audience know what they are talking about. They might have been thinking 'as long as I sound like a Shakespearian actor then nobody will ask any questions'. Invariably it turned out that this happened in sections where the actor did not really understand what they were saying.

One of the most refreshingly honest moments came when a performer (interestingly, a dancer) held his hand up and said that he did not understand Shakespeare. During the week-long session, he had to break everything down and really get his head around it before he could let the words pass his lips. In the end he gave by far the most interesting and honest performance.

Sometimes performers can hide behind the words. Or they might attack the words and hope for the best. This made us think about how we could combat this and help the performer feel comfortable with the meaning of the text, and in doing so we developed this very simple exercise. It was born of research and development for *Othello*, but it could work with other complicated monologues.

1   Give the performer some time with the text.
2   Ask them to consider and identify the subjects that are addressed within the text.
3   They can now use objects to represent those subjects. They can place them around the room or have them on their person.
4   Now present the text as a lecture. Don't act it. Keep emotion to a minimum. If it helps, use a pointy stick and a blackboard! Think of it as a PowerPoint presentation to the uninitiated.

We feel this process helps the actor to really get to grips with the task of communicating the meaning of text. It might seem simplistic, but we would be ignoring one of our primary tasks as directors if they were not communicating the words clearly.

The lecture has to be clear because its primary objective is to make people understand and not necessarily convey emotion. Despite all of the writhing and torment an emotional reading may produce, it might only tell us one thing – the character is upset. Presenting the text as a lecture gives the performer an opportunity to think about and express the many facets of the text. It is from this point of understanding that they can start to add emotion.

If we inspire people to embrace movement then great, but we don't want to be accused of encouraging people to neglect the basic techniques behind clarity of thought and presentation. Devised theatre should not lack the skill and depth of literary theatre. Otherwise it will be forever sidelined.

The VF exercise (*Tiny Dynamite*)

Tiny Dynamite (by Abi Morgan) is a very gentle play and has a strangely simple yet complex feel to it. It is mostly very intimate dialogue set over a few weeks in a late summer retreat, but underneath lies a dark and painful history that is demanding to be confronted.

Working with Vicky Featherstone was the first time we were permitted the freedom to think in detail about our performance and character work. We had always had responsibility for all aspects of the technical get-in and set-up and this took up most of our time. We spent a good deal of our performance with our technical heads on, thinking about sound levels or lighting states. As untrained actors we may have hidden in this comfort zone rather than concentrate on aspects of performance we found challenging or scary. Working on *Tiny Dynamite* as part of a co-production meant that those responsibilities were not on our shoulders any more and that Vicky's demands for actors' attainment would also apply to us!

Vicky introduced us to a very simple exercise aimed at getting us to consider deeply the intentions behind our words. It may not be unique to her but it struck us as a fundamentally valuable exercise that could apply to text and movement and therefore worthy of inclusion here.

This exercise is not about making a physical scene or necessarily about devising. It is about using physicality to unlock your understanding of an existing text and supporting the actor's performance. The exercise has very simple rules which, nonetheless, take a little bit of thinking about. It also works best with duologues.

Place two performers facing each other on a diagonal across the room. They should stand roughly ten feet apart. The exercise will use a lot of space so set out the longest possible diagonal in the room. The performers will stick rigidly to this line.

When participants are in place give them their scripts. They must read from their scripts, trying to avoid any inflection or performance quality. This will be harder than it seems. For this to work they must read their words like instructions and do no more. Any kind of naturalistic delivery or response will invalidate this exercise.

Now for the instruction that might take a little thought to complete. Ask your performers to take a step or steps towards their partner if they felt that their own words in any way showed a warmth or were sympathetic to the other character. Conversely, they should take steps away if they considered their words to be cold or unsympathetic. The decision to be made is what is the true intention or attitude behind the words. The number of steps used is an indicator of the intensity of each decision.

Look out for any natural rhythms appearing. Get the performers to fight this instinct. Using the rest of the performers/students as an audience here is very helpful. They are not watching the performance of a scene; they are watching the deconstruction of a scene into a series of decisions. We are seeing what the characters really mean when they say their words. More specifically we are watching what the performers think the characters are saying and feeling underneath. A very important stage of this is getting your audience (who would also have a knowledge of the scene) to say when they disagree with an action. They could simply and silently raise their arm when they feel they disagree with a move. You are then workshopping the scene with the whole group. This can be either enlightening or a minefield but what becomes apparent is that you are now vehemently debating the implications of single words and their intentions.

What we also have is a physical pattern played out on the floor. As the performers/characters move towards and away from each other we see the thrust and parry of their engagement. Also consider where they started and where they ended up: Are they closer at the end of the scene? Has one character forced the other into a corner? Have they been blown apart by this exchange? What implication does this have for where they start if we were to try this exercise on their next scene together?

Also, if this was a battle, then how were little victories achieved? Was it by bludgeoning their opponent into submission or was it by retreating and then exposing their weaknesses? We have often found there to be a startling strength in a tactically passive approach. This is a much more complex and pleasing discovery.

Run the exercise several times and ask your performers how the actions of the other character made them feel. Did they surprise them in any way? Have any of their own decisions changed from the last time you ran the exercise?

Remember that this exercise is about exploring the warmth and coldness of your own lines. An extension of this would be for performers to take steps based on how their character feels about the other's words. With this a performer is now thinking about the impact upon their own character.

This simple exercise opens up the text in such detail and served us so well in *Tiny Dynamite*. The physical relationship played out in the strict rules of the exercise stayed with us and reminded us of the complexity and depth behind every moment of this play. It is often so easy to glide through scenes on autopilot or to think that there are only a few obvious points where there is any significance. This exercise reminds us about the complexity of action and reaction, of how conversation can be a rich sparring session, full of little victories and devastating losses.

The important thing to remember with the exercise was that we never performed the scene. Performing it kills the exercise. Also the rules set were the ones that suited our needs with *Tiny Dynamite*. The exercise is perfectly malleable to your needs as long as your structure is clear and adhered to.

PHYSICAL CHARACTERS AND RELATIONSHIPS

These are exercises that look for the physical truth of a situation through a variety of means. Each one demonstrates a different practical device in attempting to locate this truth.

Time Passing

Think of a simple setting for two characters: on a sofa in front of a TV; in a café; a date in a restaurant. Ask your performers (or characters who inhabit the setting) to picture their moves over an extended period of time – all the changes of position and the different poses that one might get into quite naturalistically over the space of a couple of hours. If it helps to visualise it, think of a CCTV camera spying on the event and capturing the moves.

Get the two performers to set their individual moves, taking care to include moments of stillness and rest. If you then run the two individuals together in the space, a physical story emerges. There may be moments that you want to hold on to, to set. Others you might want to change.

Give your performers a section of fairly sparse dialogue from a script of your choice. Let the performers run the moves under the dialogue while the rest of the creative team look for moments where the moves and the words really work. (Look for moments that possess a pleasing dynamic relationship rather than an obvious literal relationship.)

Now encourage the performers to give plenty of space to the words, to take plenty of time. As the moves have a life of their own it might appear like this simple conversation has taken all night to run its course. Or it might suggest that the characters are very uneasy and are desperate to escape from this situation. The very least you should find is that the characters are possibly saying things that they might not believe. Their physicality is undermining their sincerity, although there might equally be moments where the movements actually enforce the sincerity. Either way what you have discovered is the important relationship between context (the café, the dialogue) and the subtext (the discomfort, the need to escape). It is a great example of how, from simple physicality, a complex subtext can emerge.

This exercise is about finding a subtext where we may have not considered one. Of course when we know our play inside out we are well aware of the subtext that runs through each scene. We can still use Time Passing to help the performers experience that subtext, even if the physical quality achieved never becomes part of the performance. It serves as a physical memory of the richness and depth beneath the text and will enhance a naturalistic performance.

Variations

Get your performers to set their moves. Now place one of the performers in 'the café'. Without saying a word they can start their moves and loop them so that we can see the repetition. What does this do? Do the moves look comfortable? Is the character practising for something?

Ian Golding and Georgina Lamb, *Dirty Wonderland*, 2005

Introduce the other character somewhere else in the café. When they are settled they can start and loop their moves. Try setting them off at a slower pace to see if anything emerges here. Do the two people, oblivious to each other, comment on one another or some mutual situation? Physically they are not now 'together' so what has this done to the emerging story or context?

Start again with the first character. Introduce the second character and place them together. What happens if only one of them speaks their side of the dialogue? What happens if they say nothing but just look into each other's eyes as their bodies act out a whole evening of naturalistic adjustments?

Can these naturalistic gestures be taken to an extreme? Is there greater movement potential in these gestures?

This is another starting point for the creation of choreography. To do this you must let your performers break free of the original framework. The moves are not naturalism now. They do not have to say more loudly what they said before. They are a new palette with which to create choreography rooted in the frustrations, desires, anxieties found in the earlier exercise. Remember that although you are now moving away from text, you have, very importantly, come from text.

Rabbit Room

Rabbit was the first production on which we started with a pre-written play and pre-existing characters (apart from *Look Back in Anger*). This seems like such a given for 'normal' theatre, but it was an exciting new departure for us.

We were wary of treating the written play as a limiting factor in the creative process. As the text was originally created for another production there was not necessarily any consideration for physical work. As the words did their job eloquently enough we wanted to explore the unsaid that might exist around them. I am sure there is a case for just letting the words do their job alone, but we felt that this script was full of barbed wit and cruelty but lacked the painful and silent responses to that wit and cruelty. We were also working with the writer on this aspect rather than working against what he had written (so that makes everything all right!).

Rabbit opens in a domestic setting. It is a plush holiday home of a very successful and domineering father figure. His estranged and rebellious

Karl Sullivan in *Rabbit*, 2003

daughter brings her drop out boyfriend over to meet the parents. The set-up struck us as one of awkwardness and tension and not necessarily words. As soon as the set was constructed in the rehearsal room we wanted to have a play with this.

We put each character into the room on their own for a few moments, just so they could get a feel for it. Each one had to explore the levels of comfort and discomfort, ownership and terror the room inflicted on them. The physical range of their naturalistic actions was startling. It was clear from the beginning of the show that they would all be coming from vastly different physical and emotional places. This might seem obvious but the exercise presented, or rather highlighted, a palette of nervous or relaxed physicality for us to play with.

The next exercise asked each performer to picture the unfolding evening for their character as a series of physical journeys. They did not have to make any great leaps to the end of the play, just consider this initial meeting and early evening dinner. Even then, they were allowed some freedom and were told not to be too literal: Do not try to tell us the whole story through your journey; just make the route mean something to you.

They were to imagine a CCTV camera charting their moves over three hours and compressing them into a one-minute physical journey. This would involve moving across the room, sitting down, maybe getting themselves a drink – all fairly naturalistic stuff. We would then ask one of them to enter the room and go through their material. They would keep looping it until instructed to stop.

Next another character would be asked to enter and they would make eye contact whenever they wanted to. They would both stick to their string of material and this would throw up some fascinating comings together and moments of tension. These were exactly the moments of the unsaid we were looking for.

We threw in another character to see how that changed things. And then another until they are all in. Then we started taking them out until we had explored all possible permutations. As each performer remained in character they found out so much about the interpersonal dynamics of the four people in the house through moments of connection that the script did not allow for. The exercise added a depth to the relationship between the angsty daughter and her boorish father. The script told us that they were once much closer and that the daughter now despises him, but these silent and charged moments suggested a complex emotional desire that existed somewhere in between those two extremities. Could she really hate him in the ways that she said? Had he really lost all hope in her? These questions were the interesting shades between the black and white of the words spoken. This is what we were looking for.

Watching from the outside is so thrilling. These random moments continued to teach us things about these characters that we just did not, and could not, know. There were hundreds of possible thoughts and opinions held by the characters.

It is dangerous to go off piste with this type of character work. What helped prevent us from exploring the pointless was having the writer in the room with us. He was watching his characters come alive in ways that he had not considered, but they were always existing within the world he had created. He could always tell us if we started to leave that world.

Some of this exercise made it into the show. A scene where they all meet in the house and chat before dinner was tightly choreographed implementing the routes found by the actors using the same format, e.g. an evening compacted into a much shorter passage of time.

We played with this exercise a little. We pushed the physicality further away from the naturalism and allowed our performers to heighten the dynamism of their journeys. They could really fly around the room, bouncing off walls and furniture if they encountered them. Characters would attract and repel, unconsciously imitate and provoke each other. The room became explosively dynamic but, interestingly, the stories and characters survived.

The final scene incorporated elements of both exercises.

The key to these exercises is knowing enough about your characters to place them in new positions and shed even more light on them. If you do not know anything about them, then you will not be surprised and challenged in the same way. Similarly your actors will not be able to contribute to such an extent if they do not have confidence in their knowledge of their characters.

Stockholm Post-Its

This task came up in the rehearsals for *Stockholm* and works well for exploring the intimate details of modern relationships. It is useful background work, but the process was so successful and enthralling to watch that we even tried to incorporate a similar scene into the show itself. (It did not survive a final cut!)

For our version we used the *Stockholm* set as it was a domestic kitchen, but it does not have to take place on set and in character. It can be an informative process in itself.

1   Split the group into pairs. Ask your performers to write ten Post-it notes to their partner or lover within the play. These could range from the mundane to the earth-shatteringly important but, more importantly, have to be the kind of thing you would commit to a Post-it note and leave for your partner to find.

2   Get the performers to take on these considerations. At what stage in their

relationship were these notes written? What would have prompted them? What would they have written?

3   In turn, get one performer from each pair to leave their notes around the set for the other to find. They then leave and the other performer enters the empty set. When this performer finds the notes they must respond appropriately for the next ten seconds. This is not a great big theatrical response. Just a moment of thought.

4   When they have found all the notes they then leave their written notes for the other performer to find and we repeat the process.

This is all about the effect the other has on them when they are not even there. It is about memory and intimate personal history. It is very much inspired by the effect of the editing and direction in the sex and post-sex scene in *Don't Look Now* by Nicolas Roeg. It is a useful character exercise in getting performers to think about the other characters they share the stage with and how they really feel about them and how they affect each other.

Here is another task from *Stockholm* that could work for other productions:

The two characters in the central relationship had to compile a track list of a CD they would create for their partner. These are the songs each individual thinks they might share and hold dear. They should both think about songs that meant something to them at different times in their relationship. This allows the performer to imagine a rich and varied backstory existing alongside popular culture. The choice of music cannot fail to suggest aspects of their characters.

They both create two separate lists and swap them. The results can be shocking and illuminating. You might want to discuss them and encourage the performers to defend their inclusions. The CDs might be the choices of the individual character or they might be the soundtrack to their love. Either way they should cast a light on what one performer thinks about the couple or their relationship. You may find that both performers have vastly differing views. This is not a problem. It just opens up discussion, as it did in *Stockholm*. Some of the choices made our blood curdle, but they were no less valid than the choices we loved. It is a character exercise for the performers and an excellent opportunity to throw up some surprises. It is also a simple and effective way of separating performer from character as the performer is not asked to list their own personal favourite tracks. They are asked to list the right tracks as their character. It would then be up to you whether they should work their way to a definitive couple CD or leave the exercise there.

In addition you could ask the performers to be more detailed. They could write out individual lists for their relationship after three months, after two years, after five years.

Playing with words: Leg of Lamb

This task is an example taken from *Stockholm* rehearsals where words are taken on in a creatively lateral way to examine their potential.

We have stated many times the importance of playing with the physical material you create. We have encouraged you to test its validity and flexibility to throw up new meaning and create new stories.

This section takes a similar approach towards text. The following is an account of an exercise from the *Stockholm* research and development. We were looking at how words might *suggest* a story rather than explicitly tell it. It was principally for us to find a way to hint at a horror lurking under a domestic bliss.

We knew that we wanted our characters to prepare a meal during the show. We also wanted to explore the suggestion of death and destruction (the characters' names were Todd and Kali ('Tod' being German for 'death', and 'Kali' the Hindu goddess of destruction).

We cobbled together a mock recipe and had a play.

1. Bone the leg of lamb. Do not strip the tough meat from the knuckle end. Cut the meat you have removed from the bone into large, rough chunks. Remember that most casseroles and stews require larger cuts. Trim fat and gristle off the meat.

2. Roast the bone and the knuckle at 225 degrees for 15 minutes, put carrots, onion, celery in a pan. Add a bay leaf and half a bottle of good red wine, drinking the rest yourself! Once you have brought it to the boil, allow it to simmer very gently for 1–2 hours. Strain the stock through a fine sieve.

3. Rinse the prunes.

4. Heat your oil in a large frying pan. Soften the garlic, onion and carrots. Add all the spices, and fry for a few more minutes. Transfer to another pot. Heat some more oil in a frying pan. Brown the meat and add to the softened vegetables.

5. Bring to the boil, then reduce immediately to a very slow simmer. Simmer for 2 hours. Add the prunes and cook for another hour. Test after this time. The meat should be extremely tender.

6. Serve with mashed potato.

Read at face value it was an instructive guide through preparing and cooking a leg of lamb with prunes. We asked one of our performers to sit at a table facing us. Another performer sat in front of her with his back to us. She read the recipe to him. Then she tried to learn it. Then she read it to him again.

Already, this makes the recipe strange but there is not necessarily another story emerging. There are more questions than answers. Who is she? Why is she relaying this recipe? Who is the man sitting in front of her? And does he want to know about this recipe? Is he bored? Has he asked her to do this?

Next time she spoke the recipe she had to change every present or future tense into the past tense.

> *'I boned out the leg. I didn't strip the tough meat from the knuckle end. Most casseroles and stews require larger cuts. I trimmed any fat or gristle off the meat.'*

> *'I browned the meat and added it to the softened vegetables.'*

> *'By this time the meat was extremely tender.'*

> *'I served it with mashed potato.'*

What emerged was quite startling. The performer was struggling with the task, which gave a methodical and deliberate tone to the words but more importantly a whole new context had emerged. This time it was a confession. To all of the startled observers it was clear that she had disposed of a body. The detail of what she had done to the meat was blood chilling. The man was taking her statement. Impassive. Professional. There was no escape for her. This was a confession and acceptance of an horrific deed.

This find was exactly what we were looking for. Not the murder story in particular but the potential to engage the audience in the telling of a complex story without explicitly using those words. We wanted to know if the couple within *Stockholm* could betray another story under the surface or scream for help as they talk about their wallpaper or the food they are going to cook.

We are in no way promoting an absurd approach. This is not about a disregard for the words. It is an exercise in how those words, just like the physicality, can tell a completely different story with just the slightest directorial adjustment.

chapter eight

Some things to think about

Some DOs and DON'Ts

DON'T make somebody become a table or chair that then gets sat on – this is not physical theatre, it is demeaning.

DON'T hold your breath when attempting particularly difficult physical movement – you need it. Breathe out during exertion.

DON'T, when working with jumps, create all that energy running through the space only to jump off both feet together in order to launch into the air – you just wasted a perfectly good run-up.

DON'T stand stock still facing the audience unless that really is what you mean to do.

DON'T stand back to back, link arms and lift one another by tilting forward – it doesn't mean anything. Honest.

DON'T treat movement any differently than text – they should operate under the same rules. A spoken sentence gets us from one point to another, is progressive, repeats only when necessary and has consequences. There is no reason why movement should not do this also.

DON'T allow language to become strange when combined with movement.

DON'T look out above the audience as soon as you begin to move. They're still there.

DON'T always aim for the end point when creating physical work. When directing, don't be afraid of withholding information to support this practice. A love duet might have started out as a fight duet that got slower and slower and vice versa. This is how interesting material gets made.

You will notice a lack of DOs in the list above. Sorry. That is just the way it is. It is much easier for us to say what you should not be doing. That is how we have learnt what we liked, just as reacting to what we are *not* has defined what we *are*. Instead we suggest some things you might like to think about:

- *The positive opportunities in making choreography with non-dancers.*

- *Making choreography using clearly defined limitations.*

- *Responding to stage directions, good and bad.*

- *Making choreography and then testing it. Workshopping the story.*

- *Music and audience manipulation.*

- *Movement and storytelling.*

- *Building blocks – we will keep banging on about the importance of these in our devising.*

- *Articulating the unsaid – when physicality can suggest a repressed subtext.*

- *Text vs movement (and what comes first?).*

- *What inspires the movement?*

- *Is movement the best way to tell this story?*

- *Movement and time passing.*

- *Making theatre from non-theatrical inspiration.*

Bibliography of inspiration

We have always championed accessibility to our creative process. This is not done to show how smart we are. If anything, it is the opposite. We were desperate to demystify the artistic creative process and show where ideas really come from and how they are shaped by the things around us.

Within our education packs we have written about process and development but at the back of each existed a simple list we called the 'Bibliography of inspiration'. In this list we laid bare the ingredients that were crucial in the genesis of the production. They were shamelessly personal and could reference the banal as easily as the highbrow.

Here are some more lists written as honestly as we can in retrospect. It is best not to look too deeply into each thing as they are so personal. We have our reasons why the things on these lists are pivotal. Without going into those reasons they just look trivial. But then that is the point we are making – inspiration comes from the oddest of places and is utterly subjective.

We hope these lists can inspire you to look a little closer to home for your own creative inspiration. If you are thrown by the lack of academic index, we would advise you to use an Internet search engine. It might throw up some unexpected and inspirational results. Go on. Live a little!

Look Back in Anger

Generation X – Douglas Coupland (Abacus, 1991)

Dennis Potter's *The Singing Detective*, *Karaoke* and *Cold Lazarus* TV series (BBC, 1986; BBC/Channel 4, 1996)

The car park we had to start rehearsals in

Reading the play and finding it was not what we thought it was. It had fire in its belly

The desire to present *Look Back in Anger* with that fire back in its belly

Klub

The Escape club, Swansea

DJ Andy Cleeton

Rave Off: Politics and Deviance in Contemporary Youth Culture – Steve Redhead (Avebury, 1993)

Hearing 'Access' by DJ Tim and DJ Misjah for the first time at the Hacienda, Manchester

Stills from the film *The Basketball Diaries* (Scott Kalvert, 1995)

Flesh

Norman Tebbit's speech about getting on your bike and looking for work

Photography of Robert Longo

Korina's visit to a Swansea butcher's shop

The title sequence from the film *Seven* (David Fincher, 1995)

Interviews with prostitutes in Swansea, London and Edinburgh

The work of Barbara Hepworth

Zero

Sitting in the back of a mini bus in Ecuador and us all thinking 'How the hell did we get here?'

Predicting pre-millennium angst

An abandoned Wendy house in the middle of our rehearsal space

A terrible New Year's Eve

A Carling lager advert where it snows

The Age of Anxiety – ed. Sarah Dunant and Roy Porter (Virago, 1996)

Children of Chaos – Douglas Rushkoff (Flamingo, 1997)

The *Children of the Damned* film (Anton Leader, 1963)
Disco dancefloor sequence in *Boogie Nights* (Paul Thomas Anderson, 1997)
Moonman's track 'Galaxia'

Sell Out

Having reached a deadline to write an Arts Council application for our new
show and 'an argument between friends gets out of hand' being the first
thing that came into our minds
Inter-company tension towards the end of the *Zero* tour
Exhibition with the light chairs by Eurolounge
The depth of spite and general nastiness emerging from the questionnaires
set by Michael Wynne
Craig Armstrong's *The Space Between Us* album (Melankolic, 1998)

Hymns

The experience of laughing when we shouldn't, e.g. at funerals
Craig Armstrong's soundtrack for *Plunkett & Maclean* (Melankolic, 1999)
Liam Steel shouting in rehearsal one day, 'Be less fighty!' He was right, but
that does not stop us laughing about it to this day
Not Guilty – David Thomas (William Morrow & Co., 1993)
Stiffed: Betrayal of Modern Man – Susan Faludi (Harper Perennial, 2000)
Enter Achilles – dance film by DV8 (BBC, 1996)
'Nothing for Ruth' – poem by Edward Lowbury
'The Snow Man' – poem by Wallace Stevens, from *Collected Poetry and Prose*
(Library of America)
'Local Boy in the Photograph' – song by Stereophonics (*Word Gets Around*,
V2 Records, 1997)
12 Angry Men (Sidney Lumet, 1957)

Underworld

Creating a show that we could not be in and would not have to tour (all female)
Also about death, it was to be a female companion piece to *Hymns* (originally
to be called *Hearse. Hymns . . . Hearse . . .* Geddit?). It was going to be a
comedy . . . with karaoke . . .
Changing our minds and making a horror for the stage
The Shining (Stanley Kubrick, 1980)

Hammer House of Horror films
T. C. Howard shouts 'Dance!'
Finding a bath in the rehearsal room
Disposing of a body in a bath
The wonders of flash paper
The effect and shock of blood on porcelain
Don't Look Now (Nicolas Roeg, 1973)
Wigan Soul Weekenders
The Lakes TV series (BBC, 1997)
The scene in the car in the traffic jam towards the end of *The Sixth Sense* (M. Night Shyamalan, 1999)
James Horner's theme tune for *Unbreakable* (Hollywood Records, 2000)
The Love Unlimited Orchestra

Tiny Dynamite

The chance to work with Vicky Featherstone and Abi Morgan
Big Brother – Channel 4 series
Summer of Love genre of movies
New England lakes
Cornelia Parker
The Darwin Awards

Heavenly

Selfishly, just wanting to have a laugh with Liam Steel
The Marx Brothers
Noises Off by Michael Frayn (believe it or not)
Crazy Gary's Mobile Disco by Gary Owen
Vicky Featherstone giving us the strength to throw away and start again
Pierre et Gilles photography

Peepshow

The video to 'Protection' by Massive Attack directed by Michel Gondry (1995)
A performer's dad saying that our work could do with a few songs
A member of the audience noting that, in a previous production, she thought that we were about to break out into song. When asked why she said 'because you could have'

The music of lamb
The twisted personality of Dan O'Neill
Having coffee with Nick Skillbeck and him saying he would work with us on it
Rear Window by Alfred Hitchcock (1954)
Michael Caine and Maggie Smith in the film *California Suite* by Herbert Ross
(1978)
The block of flats opposite the company office
The film *Italian For Beginners* by Lone Scherfig (2002)
Visiting a real peepshow in Soho
The song 'Destiny' by Zero 7 (*Simple Things*, Ultimate Dilemma, 2001)
The use of Aimee Mann's songs in the film *Magnolia* by P. T. Anderson
(Magnolia, Reprise, 1999)
'An Echo, A Stain' by Bjork (Vespertine, 2001)
Photographer Nan Goldin
Jonathan Glazer's 'Odyssey' TV advert for Levi Jeans (2002)

Rabbit

Long Weekend (Colin Eggleston, 1978)
Cat on a Hot Tin Roof (Richard Brooks, 1958)
Six Feet Under – TV series, created by Alan Ball (HBO, 2001)
Deadly Avenger – musician
Thomas Newman – composer
The Last Supper – painting, Leonardo da Vinci
Enrique Metinides – photographer
Felt Mountain (Goldfrapp, 2000) album artwork
The Corrections – Jonathan Franzen (Farrar, Straus & Giroux, 2001)
Star Wars (George Lucas, 1977)
'Ozymandias' – poem by P. B. Shelley
'There There' video for Radiohead – dir. Chris Hopwell (2000)
Pieter Claesz and the Vanitas movement

Dirty Wonderland

The dirty and wonderful music of Goldfrapp
Our desire to make a site-specific show
A high-profile theatre reviewer correctly stating that most site-specific work
was vapid
Visits to and getting thrown out of the Grand Ocean Hotel in Saltdean near
Brighton

Liam Steel as Bob, spending another birthday alone, *Dirty Wonderland*, 2005

The photography of Nan Goldin
A freaky and scary-looking waiter at the Grand Ocean Hotel
Ian Golding's parents' honeymoon
Having 200 rooms, a bar, a dining room, a ballroom and a reception to play with

pool (no water)

Nan Goldin – photography
Amadeus – Peter Shaffer (play, 1979)
Psycho (Alfred Hitchcock, 1960)
Lisa Maguire stating 'But where is the PAIN?' after seeing an early run-through
Play – Samuel Beckett (play, 1963)
Working with Imogen Heap – musician
Rubbish celebrity vox pop documentaries on Channel 4
Frankenstein/Prometheus myth (destroying your creation once it is clear it has
    become a monster)
Jacob Love – film maker
Short Cuts – Robert Altman film, 1993 (for its brilliant use of nudity to create
    an unnerving scenario)

The Swimming Pool by David Hockney – artist
Wanting to play with Mark Ravenhill
'All is Full of Love' (Bjork) – Chris Cunningham music video (2002)
Some shapes thrown by Eddie Kay in a residency in Leeds
The Cruel Elephant by David Hockney – artist
The Kingdom – Lars von Trier TV mini series (1994)
Kill Bill (Quentin Tarantino, 2003–4)
Crazy P's 'Lady T' song
Ellie Parker (Scott Coffey, 2005)
'Got 'til it's Gone' (Janet Jackson) – Mark Romanek music video (1998)
Andy Purves' strobe work
KLF Foundation – conceptual artists
The work of Ron Mueck (artist) and a subsequent article in the *Guardian*

Stockholm

The Seventh Seal (Ingmar Bergman, 1957)
Scenes from a Marriage (Ingmar Bergman, 1973)
'To Build a Home' – song by The Cinematic Orchestra (Ninja Tune, 2007)
Downfall (Oliver Hirschbiegel, 2004)
Cymbeline by William Shakespeare
The Rape of Lucrece by William Shakespeare
The Dead – James Joyce (Grant Richards, 1914)
Poltergeist (Tobe Hooper, 1982)
Don't Look Now – Nicolas Roeg, as above
Police Academy (Hugh Wilson, 1984)
Autumnal Cannibalism – Salvador Dali painting
The photographic art of Gregory Crewdson
Cover for the Beautiful South single 'We Are Each Other' (1992)